Amazingly Simple
Star Quilts™

EDITED BY
JEANNE STAUFFER & SANDRA L. HATCH

HOUSE of
WHITE
BIRCHES

PUBLISHERS
SINCE 1947

Amazingly Simple Star Quilts

EDITORS	Jeanne Stauffer, Sandra L. Hatch
ART DIRECTOR	Brad Snow
PUBLISHING SERVICES DIRECTOR	Brenda Gallmeyer
ASSOCIATE EDITOR	Dianne Schmidt
ASSISTANT ART DIRECTOR	Nick Pierce
COPY SUPERVISOR	Michelle Beck
COPY EDITORS	Sue Harvey, Nicki Lehman, Judy Weatherford
TECHNICAL ARTIST	Connie Rand
GRAPHIC ARTS SUPERVISOR	Ronda Bechinski
GRAPHIC ARTISTS	Debby Keel, Edith Teegarden
PRODUCTION ASSISTANTS	Cheryl Kempf, Marj Morgan, Judy Neuenschwander
PHOTOGRAPHY	Tammy Christian, Don Clark, Matthew Owen, Jackie Schaffel
PHOTO STYLISTS	Tammy Nussbaum, Tammy M. Smith
PUBLISHING DIRECTOR	David J. McKee
EDITORIAL DIRECTOR	Gary Richardson
MARKETING DIRECTOR	Dan Fink

Printed in China
First Printing: 2006
Library of Congress Control Number: 2005933635
Hardcover ISBN-10: 1-59217-077-3
Hardcover ISBN-13: 978-1-59217-077-7
Softcover ISBN-10: 1-59217-125-7
Softcover ISBN-13: 978-1-59217-125-5

1 2 3 4 5 6 7 8 9

Welcome

Some of our very first quilts were made with star-design blocks. Templates were made, individual pieces were cut, and they were painstakingly hand-pieced together.

As we became more experienced quilters, we learned faster and easier methods of piecing that include the use of rotary-cutting tools and quick-stitching methods. Star designs no longer require time-consuming cutting and piecing methods.

The quilts in this book were designed to use these methods; they are simple, yet stunning. Some of them still require a template or two, but all may be machine-stitched. Perfect points with tiny pieces may be achieved using paper-piecing methods as evidenced by Starburst (page 19).

Most designs are pieced, but our designers have not forgotten the appliqué enthusiasts. Starflowers Quilt (page 134) and Ahoya Flowers (page 54) add a challenge and a twist to the star design.

So what are you waiting for? Choose your favorite design, gather up the fabrics, set aside a block of time and get ready to create an amazingly simple star-design quilt today.

Warm regards,

Jeanne Stauffer

Sandra L. Hatch

Contents

Garden Stars **6**

Plenty of Stars **10**

Stars of the Forest **14**

Starburst **19**

Shooting Star **22**

Filtered Sunlight **27**

Twinkling Gold **30**

Grandmother's Stars **34**

Ocean Stars **38**

Shimmering Stars **42**

Island Sunrise **45**

Welcome Home **50**

Ahoya Flowers **54**

Shining Stars **63**

Fireworks Fancy **66**

Heavenly Stars **70**

True Colors **74**

Prairie Points Throw **77**

Stars in the Crossroads **80**

Double Star Baby Quilt **84**

Spinning Stars **87**

Starry Night **92**

Jewel of the Night **96**

Circling Stars of the Orient **103**

Woven Stars **108**

Framed Stars **112**

Back to the Fifties **116**

Stars in Flight **121**

The Stars Inside **124**

Star Rockets in Flight **129**

Starflowers Quilt **134**

Homespun Stars **138**

Four-Patch Galaxy **142**

Zuma Sky **146**

Kaleidoscope Stars **152**

Yo-Yo Star Table Topper **162**

Morning Star **166**

GENERAL INSTRUCTIONS **173**   SPECIAL THANKS **176**   FABRICS & SUPPLIES **176**

Garden Stars
10" x 10" Block

DESIGN BY
CONNIE KAUFMANN

Garden Stars

Fabric flowers bloom on a star background in this colorful wall quilt.

Project Specifications

Skill Level: Intermediate
Quilt Size: 39½" x 39½"
Block Size: 10" x 10"
Number of Blocks: 9

Fabric & Batting

- ⅛ yard each purple, light purple, pale purple, pink, orange, peach, blue, yellow and burgundy florals
- ⅜ yard yellow dot
- ⅜ yard light green dot
- ⅝ yard green plaid
- ¾ yard blue mottled
- ⅞ yard dark green mottled
- Backing 46" x 46"
- Batting 46" x 46"

Supplies & Tools

- All-purpose thread to match fabrics
- Quilting thread
- Triangulations 2.0 CD-ROM (optional)
- Basic sewing tools and supplies

Cutting

Step 1. Cut one 2½" by fabric width strip yellow dot; subcut strip into nine 2" A squares.

Step 2. Cut four 1¾" by fabric width strips yellow dot for J borders.

Step 3. Cut three 2½" by fabric width strips light green dot; subcut strips into (36) 2½" B squares.

Step 4. If using the Triangulations 2.0 CD-ROM, print six pages of 2" finished half-square triangles (enough to make 72 half-square triangle units). Print two pages of 1" finished half-square triangles; cut the paper into nine pieces that will each make four half-square triangles.

Step 5. If using papers, cut fabric strips large enough to cover the 2" finished half-square triangle papers from blue (G) and dark green (H) mottleds. If not, cut three 2⅞" by fabric width strips each blue (G) and dark green (H) mottleds; subcut strips into (36) 2⅞" squares of each fabric. Draw a diagonal line from corner to corner on the wrong side of each G square.

Step 6. From each floral fabric, cut four 2½" x 2½" C squares.

Step 7. If using papers, cut a D fabric strip large

Step 10. Cut four 1" by fabric width K strips dark green mottled.

Step 11. Cut four 4" by fabric width L strips green plaid.

Step 12. Cut five 2¼" by fabric width strips dark green mottled for binding.

Completing the Blocks

Step 1. If using printed papers, layer a floral D strip and one E strip with right sides together. Place a 1" finished half-square triangle paper over the layered fabrics; pin in place. Sew along the sewing lines on the paper.

Step 2. Cut out along the cutting lines to make eight D-E units; press seams toward D.

Step 3. Repeat Steps 2 and 3 with H and G strips to complete eight H-G units; press seams toward H.

Step 4. If not using papers, layer a D square with an E square with right sides together. Stitch ¼" on each side of the marked line as shown in Figure 1; cut apart on the drawn line to complete two D-E units. Repeat to complete eight same-fabric D-E units for one block and 36 total for the quilt.

Step 5. Repeat Step 4 with the G and H squares to make G-H units, again referring to Figure 1.

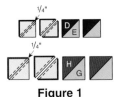

Figure 1

Step 6. To complete one block, sew A between two C squares as shown in Figure 2; press seams toward C. Sew C between two B squares; press seams toward C; repeat for two B-C-B rows, again referring to Figure 2.

Figure 2

Step 7. Sew the C-A-C row between the two B-C-B rows to complete the block center; press seams away from the C-A-C row.

Step 8. Join two same-fabric D-E units as shown

enough to cover the 1" finished half-square triangle paper from each floral. If not, cut four 1⅞" x 1⅞" squares from each floral for D.

Step 8. If using papers, cut a blue mottled E fabric strip large enough to cover each of the 1" finished half-square triangle papers. If not, cut two 1⅞" by fabric width strips blue mottled; subcut strips into (36) 1⅞" squares for E. Draw a diagonal line from corner to corner on the wrong side of each square.

Step 9. Cut four 2½" by fabric width strips blue mottled; subcut strips into (36) 1½" F rectangles and (36) 2½" I squares.

in Figure 3; press seams in one direction. Add F to complete a D-E-F unit as shown in Figure 4; press seam toward F. Repeat for four units.

Figure 3

Figure 4

Step 9. Sew a D-E-F unit between two G-H units to make a side row as shown in Figure 5; press seams toward G-H units. Repeat for four side rows.

Figure 5

Step 10. Sew a side row to opposite sides of the block center as shown in Figure 6; press seams toward the block center.

Figure 6

Step 11. Sew I to each end of each remaining side row as shown in Figure 7. Sew these rows to the remaining sides of the block center to complete one block; press seams away from the block center.

Figure 7

Step 12. Repeat Steps 6–11 to complete one block in each floral for a total of nine blocks.

Completing the Top

Step 1. Arrange blocks to make three rows of three blocks each referring to the Placement Diagram for positioning.

Step 2. Join blocks in rows; press seams in one direction. Join rows to complete the pieced center; press seams in one direction.

Step 3. Fold each K strip in half along length with wrong sides together; press.

Step 4. Place a K strip on each J strip with raw edges even; baste to hold in place.

Step 5. Sew an L strip to each J-K strip; press seams toward L.

Step 6. Center and stitch a J-K-L strip to each side of the pieced center, beginning and ending ¼" from corners of the pieced centers and mitering corners as shown in Figure 8. Trim seams at mitered corners to ¼"; press seams open. Press border seams toward J-K-L strips to complete the top.

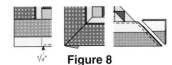
¼"   **Figure 8**

Step 7. Complete the quilt referring to Completing Your Quilt on page 175. ★

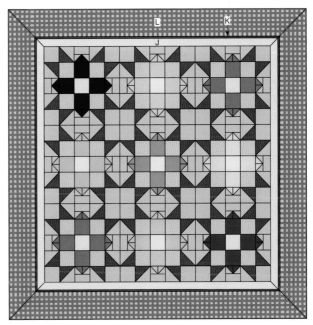
Garden Stars
Placement Diagram
39½" x 39½"

Plenty of Stars
12" x 12" Block

DESIGN BY
CONNIE RAND

Plenty of Stars

More stars appear when these paper-pieced blocks are put together.

Project Specifications
Skill Level: Intermediate
Quilt Size: 58" x 70"
Block Size: 12" x 12"
Number of Blocks: 20

Fabric & Batting
- 1½ yards yellow print
- 1⅞ yards gold print
- 2 yards dark purple print
- Backing 64" x 76"
- Batting 64" x 76"

Supplies & Tools
- All-purpose thread to match fabrics
- Quilting thread
- Basic sewing tools and supplies

Cutting
Step 1. Cut two 1½" x 60½" C strips and two 1½" x 50½" D strips along length of gold print.
Step 2. Cut two 4½" by 62½" E strips and two 4½" x 58½" F strips along length of dark purple print.
Step 3. Cut four 2¼" strips along length of dark

purple print for binding.
Step 4. Refer to Basic Paper Piecing in the General Instructions to cut fabrics for paper-pieced blocks.

Completing the Paper-Pieced Blocks
Step 1. Make 80 copies each of Paper-Piecing Patterns A and B; cut out, leaving paper beyond the outside line of each pattern.
Step 2. Complete 80 A units and 80 B units referring to Basic Paper Piecing in the General Instructions on page 173 and Figures 1–4.

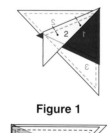

Figure 1

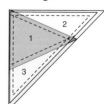

Figure 2

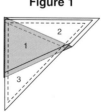

Figure 3

Figure 4

Completing the Top

Step 1. Join four blocks to make a row as shown in Figure 8; press seams in one direction. Join rows to complete the pieced center referring to the Placement Diagram; press seams in one direction.

Figure 8

Step 2. Sew C strips to opposite sides and D strips to the top and bottom of the pieced center; press seams toward C and D strips.

Step 3. Sew E strips to opposite sides and F strips to the top and bottom of the pieced center; press seams toward E and F strips to complete the pieced top.

Step 4. Remove paper backing from blocks.

Step 5. Complete the quilt referring to Completing Your Quilt on page 175. ★

Step 3. To piece one block, join one each A and B unit to make a quarter-block unit as shown in Figure 5; press seam toward the B unit. Repeat for four quarter-block units.

Figure 5

Step 4. Join two quarter-block units to make a half-block unit as shown in Figure 6; repeat. Press seams toward the A units.

Figure 6

Figure 7

Step 5. Join the two half-block units to complete the block; split seam in center and press toward A units as shown in Figure 7 to complete one block. Repeat for 20 blocks.

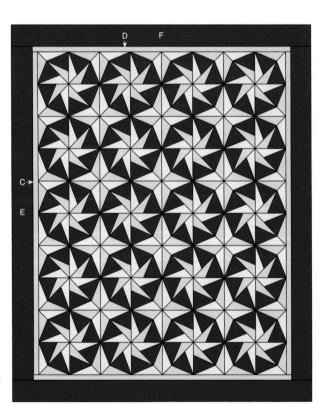

Plenty of Stars
Placement Diagram
58" x 70"

Paper-Piecing Pattern A
Make 80 copies

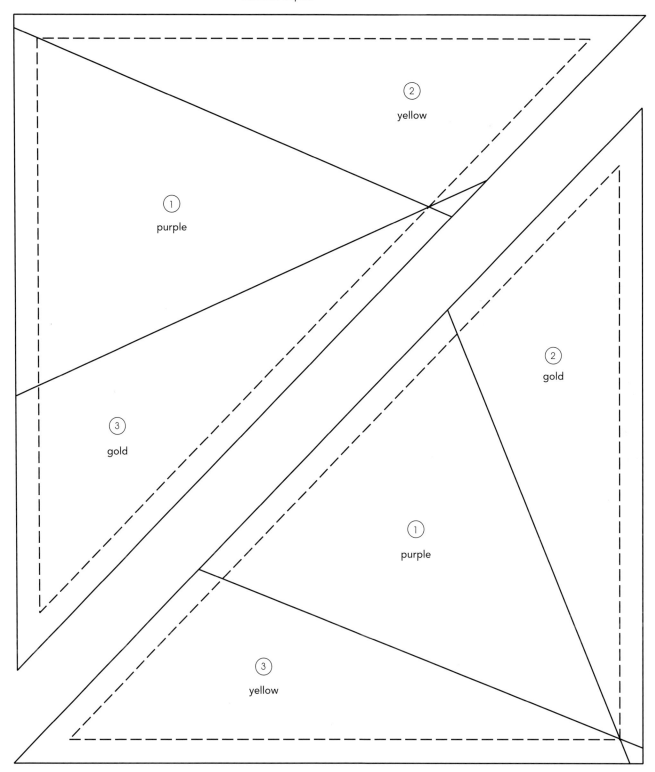

① purple

② yellow

③ gold

② gold

① purple

③ yellow

Paper-Piecing Pattern B
Make 80 copies

Star of the Forest A
12" x 12" Block

Star of the Forest B
12" x 12" Block

DESIGN BY
SUE HARVEY

Stars of the Forest

Pieced trees emerge from all sides of the center star in this pillow set.

Project Specifications

Skill Level: Intermediate
Pillow Size: 18" x 18"
Block Size: 12" x 12"
Number of Blocks: 2

Fabric & Batting

- Fat quarter cream plaid
- Fat quarter brown print
- Fat quarter each medium and dark green plaids
- ⅜ yard dark green plaid for binding
- ½ yard gold stripe
- 1⅛ yards green print
- Lining (2) 24" x 24"
- Batting (2) 24" x 24"

Supplies & Tools

- Neutral color all-purpose thread
- Quilting thread
- Basting spray
- 2 (18" x 18") pillow forms
- Basic sewing tools and supplies

Cutting

Step 1. Cut five 1½" x 22" strips cream plaid; subcut into two 1½" A squares, eight 1½" M squares, (16) 2½" H rectangles and eight 3" O rectangles.

Step 2. Cut one 1¾" x 22" strip cream plaid; subcut into eight 1¾" C squares.

Step 3. Cut two 2¼" x 22" strips cream plaid; subcut into (16) 2¼" J squares.

Step 4. Cut two 1½" x 22" strips brown print; subcut into eight 1¾" B rectangles and eight 1½" G squares.

Step 5. Cut two 3" x 22" strips brown print; subcut into eight 3" I squares.

Step 6. Cut two 5½" x 22" strips medium green plaid; subcut into eight 3" F rectangles.

Step 7. Cut three 3" x 22" strips dark green plaid; subcut into eight 1½" L rectangles and (12) 3" N squares.

Step 8. Cut one 1¾" x 22" strip dark green plaid; subcut into four 1¾" K squares.

Step 9. Cut two 3" by fabric width strips gold stripe; subcut into (16) 3" E squares.

Step 10. Cut four 1½" by fabric width strips gold stripe; subcut into four each 12½" P strips and 14½" Q strips.

Step 3. Sew B between two C squares, again referring to Figure 2; press seams toward B. Repeat for four C strips.

Step 4. Sew an A strip between two C strips to complete one Nine-Patch unit as shown in Figure 3; press seams toward the C strips. Repeat for two units.

Figure 3

Step 5. Sew D to each side of the Nine-Patch units to complete the block center units as shown in Figure 4; press seams toward D.

Figure 4

Step 6. Place an E square right sides together on one end of F referring to Figure 5 for correct positioning of stripe; stitch on the marked line, trim seam allowance to ¼" and press E open, again referring to Figure 5. Repeat with E on the remaining end of F, again referring to Figure 5 for positioning of stripe. Repeat to complete eight E-F units.

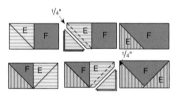

Figure 5

Step 7. Sew G between two H rectangles as shown in Figure 6; press seams toward G. Repeat for eight G-H units.

Figure 6   **Figure 7**

Step 8. Sew a G-H unit to the F side of each E-F unit to complete eight block side units as shown in Figure 7; press seams toward G-H.

Step 11. Cut one 3⅜" by fabric width strip green print; subcut into four 3⅜" squares. Cut each square in half on one diagonal to make eight D triangles.

Step 12. Cut four 2½" by fabric width strips green print; subcut into four each 14½" R strips and 18½" S strips.

Step 13. Cut four 12" x 18½" rectangles green print for backing pieces.

Step 14. Cut four 2¼" by fabric width strips dark green plaid for binding.

Piecing Units

Step 1. Draw a diagonal line from corner to corner on the wrong side of each E, J, K, M and N square referring to Figure 1 for correct positioning of line on E squares.

Figure 1

Step 2. Sew A between two B rectangles as shown in Figure 2; press seams toward B. Repeat for two A strips.

Figure 2

Step 9. Place J right sides together on one corner of I as shown in Figure 8; stitch, trim and press J open, again referring to Figure 8. Repeat with J on the opposite corner of I to complete one I-J unit, again referring to Figure 8. Repeat to complete eight I-J units.

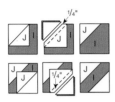

Figure 8

Completing the Blocks

Step 1. To complete the Star of the Forest A block, place N on one corner of an I-J unit as shown in Figure 9; stitch, trim and press N open to complete one trunk unit, again referring to Figure 9. Repeat to complete four trunk units.

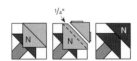

Figure 9   **Figure 10**

Step 2. Sew O to each N side of each trunk unit as shown in Figure 10; press seams toward O.

Step 3. Place N right sides together on the open corner of a pieced unit as shown in Figure 11; stitch, trim and press N open to complete one tree corner unit, again referring to Figure 11. Repeat to complete four tree corner units.

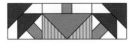 

Figure 11   **Figure 12**

Step 4. Sew a block side unit to opposite sides of the block center units to make two center rows as shown in Figure 12; press seams toward the side units. Set aside one row for block B.

Step 5. Sew a tree corner unit to opposite sides of a block side unit to make a side row referring to Figure 13; press seams toward the side unit. Repeat for two rows.

Figure 13

Step 6. Join the rows to complete the Star of the Forest A block referring to the block drawing for positioning of rows.

Step 7. To complete the Star of the Forest B block, place K on one corner of an I-J unit as shown in Figure 14; stitch, trim and press K open to complete one trunk unit, again referring to Figure 14. Repeat to complete four trunk units.

Figure 14

Step 8. Place M right sides together on one end of L as shown in Figure 15; stitch, trim and press M open, again referring to Figure 15. Repeat for two L-M units. Repeat to complete two reversed L-M units, again referring to Figure 15.

Figure 15   **Figure 16**

Step 9. Sew an L-M and reversed L-M unit to the K sides of each trunk unit as shown in Figure 16; press seams toward L-M.

Step 10. Place N right sides together on the open corner of a pieced unit as shown in Figure 17; stitch, trim and press N open to complete one tree corner unit, again referring to Figure 17. Repeat to complete four tree corner units.

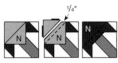

Figure 17

Figure 18

Step 11. Sew a tree corner unit to opposite sides of a block side unit to make a side row as shown in Figure 18; press seams toward the side unit. Repeat for two rows.

Step 12. Join the side rows with the remaining center row to complete the Star of the Forest B block referring to the block drawing for positioning of rows.

Completing the Pillows

Step 1. Sew P to opposite sides and Q to the remaining sides of the blocks; press seams toward strips.

Step 2. Sew R to opposite sides and S to the remaining sides to complete the tops; press seams toward strips.

Step 3. Sandwich the batting between the completed tops and prepared lining pieces using basting spray to hold layers together.

Step 4. Quilt as desired; trim batting and lining even with the quilted tops.

Step 5. Turn under one 18½" edge of each backing piece ¼" and press. Turn under again ½" and stitch to hem.

Step 6. Place a quilted top right side down; place two backing pieces wrong sides together with the quilted top with hemmed edges overlapped approximately 4" to align edges of backing pieces with edges of quilted top as shown in Figure 19; pin all around to hold. Trim edges of backing even with top, if necessary. Machine-baste ⅛" from edges; remove pins. Repeat with second top.

Figure 19

Step 7. Join the binding strips on short ends with diagonal seams to make a long strip; press seams toward one side.

Step 8. Press the strip in half along length with wrong sides together to complete the binding strip. Bind edges of each pillow cover.

Step 9. Insert pillow form through opening in back to finish. ★

Star of the Forest A Pillow
Placement Diagram
18" x 18"

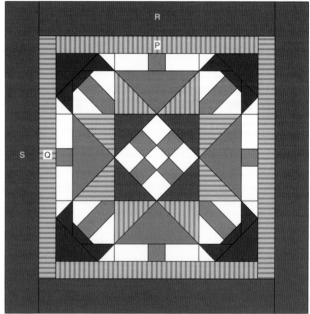

Star of the Forest B Pillow
Placement Diagram
18" x 18"

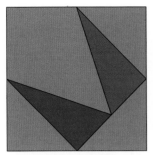

Medium Purple Starburst
4" x 4" Block
Make 8

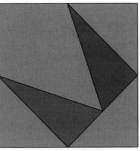

Light Purple Starburst
4" x 4" Block
Make 12

Navy Starburst
4" x 4" Block
Make 8

Purple Starburst
4" x 4" Block
Make 8

DESIGN BY
CONNIE KAUFFMAN

Starburst

Stitch accurate points using paper-pieced units.

Project Specifications
Skill Level: Intermediate
Quilt Size: 31" x 31"
Block Size: 4" x 4"
Number of Blocks: 36

Fabric & Batting
- ¼ yard each light, medium and dark purple tonals
- ½ yard navy dot
- ½ yard brown print
- ⅞ yard gold mottled
- Backing 37" x 37"
- Batting 37" x 37"

Supplies & Tools
- All-purpose thread to match fabrics
- Quilting thread
- Basic sewing tools and supplies

Cutting
Step 1. Cut three 4½" by fabric width strips brown print; subcut strips into (24) 2½" A strips and (24) 2" E strips.
Step 2. Cut one 2½" by fabric width strip navy dot; subcut strip into four 2½" B squares and eight 2" C pieces.

Step 3. Cut four 2" x 2" D squares light purple tonal.
Step 4. Prepare 36 copies of the paper-piecing pattern given. Mark eight patterns to include navy points and dark purple corner and eight to include dark purple points and navy corner. Mark 20 patterns to have medium and light purple points and brown corner.
Step 5. Cut four 2¼" by fabric width strips navy dot for binding.

Completing the Blocks
Step 1. Complete a total of 36 blocks using the paper patterns and referring to the General Instructions for paper piecing on page 173, and to the block drawings for color placement. Trim to outer line on patterns; press.

Completing the Top
Step 1. Arrange blocks in rows with two A and two E strips as shown in Figure 1; join to make six block rows. Press seams toward A and E strips.
Step 2. Join six A strips with two B and two C pieces to make an A-B-C

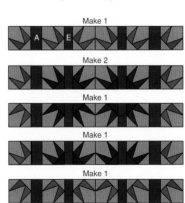

Make 1

Make 2

Make 1

Make 1

Make 1

Figure 1

sashing row as shown in Figure 2; repeat for two A-B-C sashing rows. Press seams toward A strips.

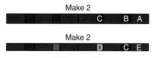

Figure 2

Step 3. Join six E pieces with two C and two D pieces to make a C-D-E sashing row, again referring to Figure 2; repeat for two C-D-E sashing rows. Press seams toward E.

Step 4. Arrange and join the block rows with the sashing rows as shown in Figure 3; press seams toward sashing rows to complete the top.

Figure 3

Step 5. Remove paper backing from blocks.

Step 6. Complete the quilt referring to Completing Your Quilt on page 175. ★

Starburst
Placement Diagram
31" x 31"

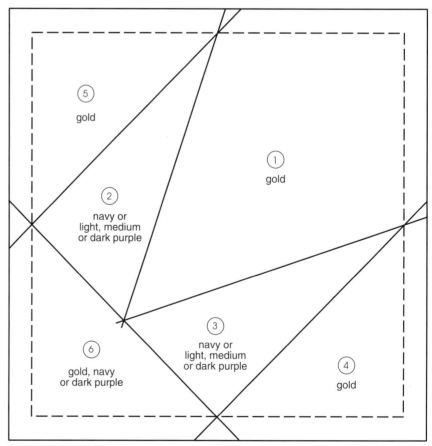

Star Blocks
Paper-Piecing Pattern
Make 36 copies

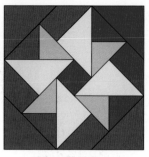

Shooting Star
9" x 9" Block

DESIGN BY
SUE REEVES

Shooting Star

One star shines brightly in a night sky created using hand-dyed fabric squares in a grid formation.

Project Specifications

Skill Level: Advanced
Quilt Size: 36" x 36"
Block Size: 9" x 9"
Number of Blocks: 1

Fabric & Batting

Hand-dyed fabrics used throughout.
- ⅛ yard orange
- ¼ yard each red and yellow/orange
- ⅓ yard each yellow and maroon
- ⅜ yard orange/yellow
- 1⅓ yards charcoal
- Backing 42" x 42"
- Batting 42" x 42"

Supplies & Tools

- Neutral color all-purpose thread
- Quilting thread
- 2¾ yards 1"-gridded fusible interfacing
- Basic sewing tools and supplies

Cutting

Step 1. Prepare templates for pieces A–E using patterns given; cut as directed on each piece.

Step 2. Cut one 2" by fabric width strip yellow; subcut strip into (18) 2" squares.

Step 3. Cut one 2¼" x 30" strip yellow; set aside for binding.

Step 4. Cut (16) 2" by fabric width strips charcoal; subcut strips into (327) 2" squares.

Step 5. Cut three 2¼" by fabric width strips charcoal; set aside for binding.

Step 6. Cut one 2" by fabric width strip each orange and red; subcut strips into 16 orange and 19 red 2" squares.

Step 7. Cut three strips each yellow/orange and orange/yellow and four strips maroon 2" by fabric width; subcut into 45 yellow/orange, 51 orange/yellow and 64 maroon 2" squares.

Completing the Block

Step 1. Sew a red C to an orange/yellow C on the short side referring to Figure 1; press seam toward red C. Repeat for two red C units. Repeat with orange/yellow and charcoal C triangles to make two charcoal C units, again referring to Figure 1.

Make 2   Make 2

Figure 1

Step 2. Add B to the C units referring to Figure 2; press seams toward B.

Figure 2

Step 3. Sew D to the B side of a B-C unit to complete a D unit as shown in Figure 3; press seams toward D. Repeat for four D units, again referring to Figure 3.

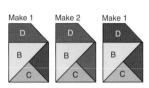

Figure 3

Figure 4

Step 4. Sew a D unit to E, matching the end of B to E and sewing a partial seam, stopping stitching ½" from end of seam as shown in Figure 4; press seam toward E.

Step 5. Add a second D unit to the C/E side of the pieced unit as shown in Figure 5; press seams toward C/E.

Figure 5   **Figure 6**

Step 6. Continue to add D units to each side of E until you reach the beginning point; press seams toward C/E. Complete partial seam as shown in Figure 6.

Step 7. Add A to each side of the pieced unit to complete the block referring to the block drawing for color placement; press seams toward A.

Completing the Top

Step 1. Cut two 50" by fabric width strips gridded

fusible web; place side by side with edges butted. Trim the interfacing on horizontal and vertical lines to make a 48" x 48" square with 48 full grid squares across and 48 down.

Step 2. Lay out all 2" squares on the interfacing pieces referring to Figure 7 and the Color Key for color order; fuse shapes in place referring to the manufacturer's instructions. ***Note:*** *Each fabric square will cover 4 grid squares (Photo 1). The edges of the fabric squares should align with grid lines on the interfacing.*

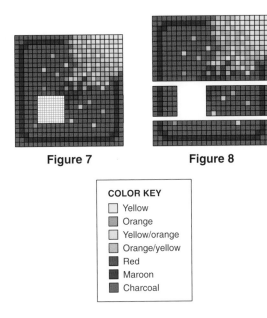

Figure 7   **Figure 8**

COLOR KEY
- ☐ Yellow
- ▨ Orange
- ☐ Yellow/orange
- ▨ Orange/yellow
- ■ Red
- ■ Maroon
- ▨ Charcoal

Step 3. Cut the fused piece into sections as shown in Figure 8; discard the plain interfacing square.

Step 4. To stitch the gridded sections, begin with one section by folding along grid lines between fabric squares with right sides together (Photo 2); stitch with a ¼" seam allowance. Stitch all horizontal seams and press (Photo 3); repeat with vertical seams and press (Photo 4).

Step 5. Lay out the stitched sections with the block referring to the Placement Diagram for positioning; join in rows. Join the rows to complete the pieced top.

Step 6. Prepare quilt layers and quilt referring to Completing Your Quilt on page 175; trim batting and backing edges even with quilted top.

Step 7. Prepare separate charcoal and yellow binding strips referring to Completing Your Quilt on page 175.

Step 8. Stitch charcoal binding to quilt edges beginning on bottom edge of quilt. Join yellow binding to charcoal binding with straight seam at orange/yellow square on top edge of quilt and continue to orange/yellow square on left edge of quilt.

Step 9. Join the charcoal strip to the yellow strip and finish binding to complete the quilt. ★

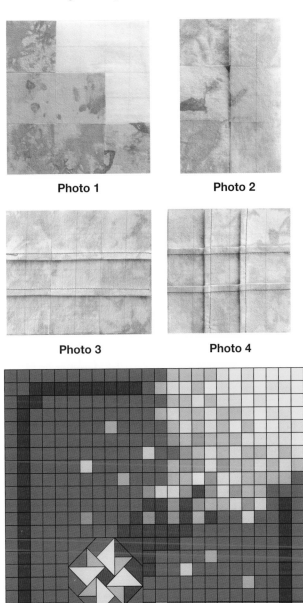

Photo 1   **Photo 2**

Photo 3   **Photo 4**

Shooting Star
Placement Diagram
36" x 36"

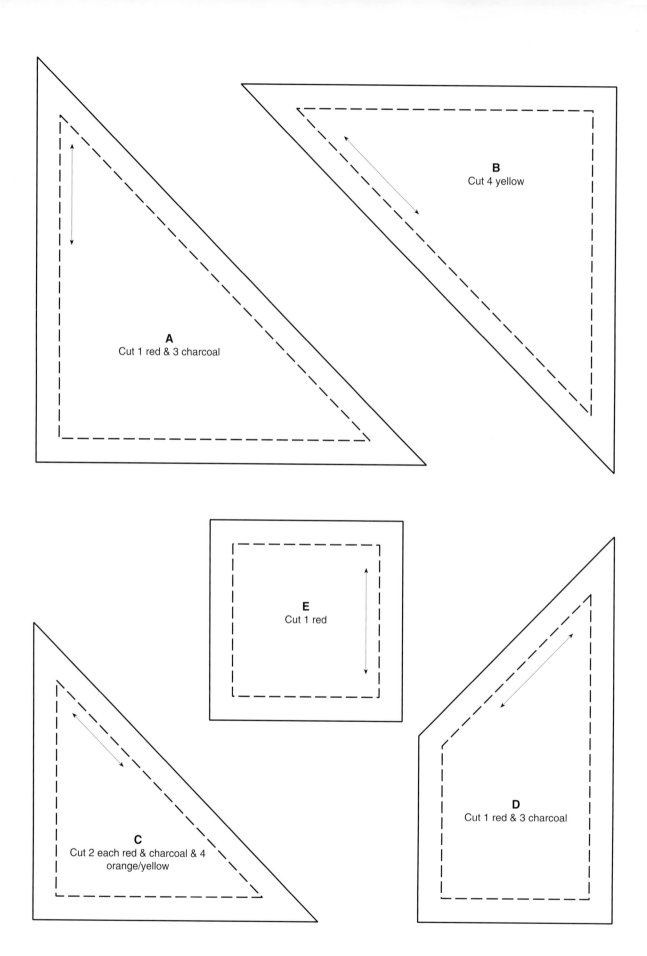

A
Cut 1 red & 3 charcoal

B
Cut 4 yellow

E
Cut 1 red

C
Cut 2 each red & charcoal & 4 orange/yellow

D
Cut 1 red & 3 charcoal

Rust Filtered Sunlight
18" x 18" Block
Make 6

Blue Filtered Sunlight
18" x 18" Block
Make 6

DESIGN BY
JUDITH SANDSTROM

Filtered Sunlight
Earth tones create the star designs in this snuggly lap-size quilt.

Project Specifications
Skill Level: Beginner
Quilt Size: 54" x 72"
Block Size: 18" x 18"
Number of Blocks: 12

Fabric & Batting
- ⅞ yard cream tonal
- 1 yard peach mottled
- 1⅓ yards rust tonal
- 1⅜ yards gray mottled
- 1½ yards light blue print
- Backing 60" x 78"
- Batting 60" x 78"

Supplies & Tools
- All-purpose thread to match fabrics
- Quilting thread
- Basic sewing tools and supplies

Cutting
Step 1. Cut one 4¾" by fabric width strip each cream tonal (A) and peach mottled (H); subcut strips into six 4¾" squares each for A and H.

Step 2. Cut three strips cream tonal (D) and two strips each light blue print (G) and rust tonal (K) 7¼" by fabric width; subcut D strips into (12) 7¼" squares and G and K strips into six each 7¼" squares. Cut each square from corner to corner on both diagonals to make 48 D and 24 each G and K triangles.

Step 3. Cut three strips rust tonal (L), five strips each peach mottled (E) and light blue print (F) and 10 strips gray mottled (B) 3⅞" by fabric width; subcut strips into 24 L, 48 each E and F and 96 B 3⅞" squares. Cut each square from corner to corner on one diagonal to make 48 L, 96 each E and F and 192 B triangles.

Step 4. Cut two strips each peach mottled (I) and gray mottled (J) and four strips light blue print (C) 3½" by fabric width; subcut strips into 24 each I and J and 48 C 3½" squares.

Step 5. Cut seven 2¼" by fabric width strips rust tonal for binding.

Completing the Blocks
Step 1. To complete one blue block, sew B to each

side of A as shown in Figure 1 to complete a center unit; press seams toward B.

Figure 1　　　　**Figure 2**

Step 2. Sew B to each short side of G and F to each short side of D to complete a B-G and an F-D unit as shown in Figure 2; press seams toward B and F.

Step 3. Join the B-G unit with the F-D unit to complete a side unit as shown in Figure 3; press seams toward the B-G unit. Repeat for four side units.

Figure 3　　　　**Figure 4**

Step 4. Sew F to E along the diagonal; press seam toward F. Repeat for two E-F units.

Step 5. Join the E-F units with two C squares as shown in Figure 4 to complete a corner unit; press seams toward C and then in one direction. Repeat for four corner units.

Step 6. Sew a side unit to opposite sides of the center unit to make the center row as shown in Figure 5; press seams toward side units.

Figure 5　　　　　**Figure 6**

Step 7. Sew a corner unit to opposite sides of each remaining side unit as shown in Figure 6 to complete the top and bottom rows; press seams toward side units.

Step 8. Join the rows to complete one blue block as shown in Figure 7; press seams in one direction. Repeat for six blue blocks.

Figure 7

Step 9. Repeat Steps 1–7 referring to Figure 8 to complete center, side and corner units to complete six rust blocks.

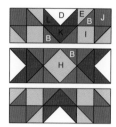

Figure 8

Completing the Top

Step 1. Join two rust blocks with one blue block to make a rust row; repeat for two rust rows. Press seams toward blue block.

Step 2. Join two blue blocks with one rust block to make a blue row; repeat for two blue rows. Press seams toward blue blocks.

Step 3. Join the rows referring to the Placement Diagram to complete the pieced top; press seams in one direction.

Step 4. Complete the quilt referring to Completing Your Quilt on page 175. ★

Filtered Sunlight
Placement Diagram
54" x 72"

Twinkling Gold
18" x 18" Block

DESIGN BY
JULIA DUNN

Twinkling Gold

Paper piecing makes short work of stitching these uneven star points.

Project Specifications
Skill Level: Intermediate
Quilt Size: 46" x 46"
Block Size: 18" x 18"
Number of Blocks: 4

Fabric & Batting
- ¼ yard gold tonal
- 1¼ yards light gold metallic
- 1½ yards cream solid
- 1½ yards dark gold mottled
- Backing 52" x 52"
- Batting 52" x 52"

Supplies & Tools
- All-purpose thread to match fabrics
- Quilting thread
- Paper
- Basic sewing tools and supplies

Cutting
Step 1. Cut two 2½" x 36½" A strips and two 2½" x 40½" B strips light gold metallic along the length of the fabric; set aside for inner borders.

Step 2. Cut two 3½" x 40½" C strips and two 3½" x 46½" D strips dark gold mottled along the length of the fabric; set aside for outer borders.

Step 3. Cut four 2¼" strips dark gold mottled along the length of the fabric for binding.

Step 4. Prepare paper-piecing patterns using patterns given. Cut fabric pieces from remaining dark gold mottled and light gold metallic for all patterns referring to Basic Paper Piecing in the General Instructions on page 173.

Step 5. Cut two 3" by fabric width strips gold tonal; subcut strips into (20) 3" F squares.

Step 6. Cut five 3½" by fabric width strips cream solid; subcut strips into (80) 2½" E pieces.

Step 7. Cut five 2¼" by fabric width strips cream solid; subcut strips into (80) 2¼" G squares.

Step 8. Cut three 6¾" by fabric width strips cream solid; subcut strips into (16) 6¾" H squares.

Completing the Blocks
Step 1. Using the paper patterns and the H squares for section 1, paper-piece a total of 16 large star-point

Step 4. Join the rows to complete one small star unit; press seams toward the center row.

Step 5. Arrange small star units with four large star-point units in rows referring to Figure 2; join to complete rows. Press seams toward large star points.

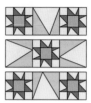

Figure 2

Step 6. Join the rows to complete one block; press seams toward the center row. Repeat for four blocks. Remove paper pieces.

units referring to Basic Paper Piecing in the General Instructions on page 173. Trim to correct line on patterns; press.

Step 2. Using the paper patterns and the E pieces for section 1, paper-piece a total of 40 small star-point units and 40 small star-point units reversed. Trim to correct line on patterns; press.

Step 3. Arrange the small star-point units with F and G pieces in rows referring to Figure 1; join to complete rows. Press seams toward F and G pieces.

Figure 1

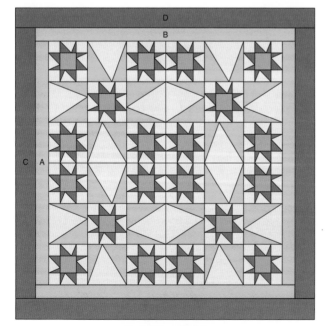

Twinkling Gold
Placement Diagram
46" x 46"

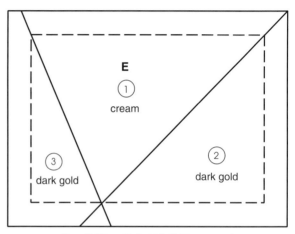

Small Star-Point Unit Reversed
Paper-Piecing Pattern
Make 40 copies

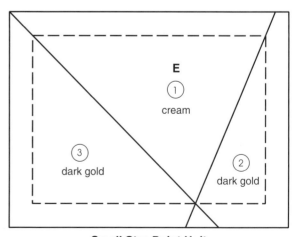

Small Star-Point Unit
Paper-Piecing Pattern
Make 40 copies

Completing the Top

Step 1. Join two blocks to make a row; repeat for two rows. Press seams in one direction.

Step 2. Join the two rows with seams in opposite directions to complete the pieced center; press seam in one direction.

Step 3. Sew an A strip to opposite sides and B strips to the top and bottom of the pieced center; press seams toward A and B strips.

Step 4. Sew a C strip to opposite sides and D strips to the top and bottom of the pieced center; press seams toward C and D strips.

Step 5. Complete the quilt referring to Completing Your Quilt on page 175. ★

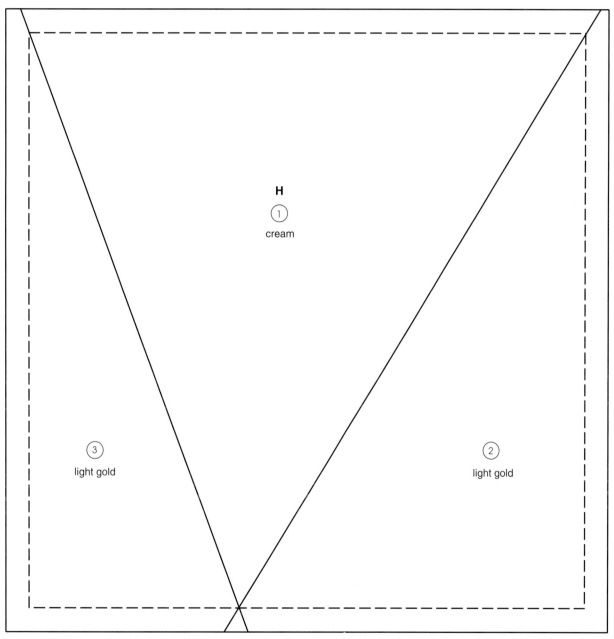

Large Star-Point Unit
Paper-Piecing Pattern
Make 16 copies

Grandmother's Stars
12" x 12" Block

DESIGN BY
JULIE WEAVER

Grandmother's Stars

Use fabrics from your grandmother's era in a table cover to remind you of her.

Project Specifications
Skill Level: Beginner
Quilt Size: 60" x 60"
Block Size: 12" x 12"
Number of Blocks: 12

Fabric & Batting
- ⅝ yard yellow dot
- 1 yard red print
- 1½ yards green dot
- 2⅞ yards cream floral
- Backing 66" x 66"
- Batting 66" x 66"

Supplies & Tools
- All-purpose thread to match fabrics
- Quilting thread
- Basic sewing tools and supplies

Cutting
Step 1. Cut one 22½" x 22½" A square cream floral.
Step 2. Cut two 1" x 22½" B strips and two 1" x 23½" C strips yellow dot.

Step 3. Cut two 1" x 23½" D strips and two 1" x 24½" E strips red print.
Step 4. Cut five 1" by fabric width strips red print. Join strips on short ends to make one long strip; press seams in one direction. Subcut strip into two 48½" F strips and two 49½" G strips.
Step 5. Cut five 1" by fabric width strips yellow dot. Join strips on short ends to make one long strip; press seams in one direction. Subcut strip into two 49½" H strips and two 50½" I strips.
Step 6. Cut six 5½" by fabric width strips cream floral. Join strips on short ends to make one long strip; press seams in one direction. Subcut strip into two 50½" J strips and two 60½" K strips.
Step 7. Cut two 4½" by fabric width strips yellow dot; subcut strips into (12) 4½" L squares.
Step 8. Cut three 2" by fabric width strips red print; subcut strips into (48) 2" M squares.
Step 9. Cut six 2½" by fabric width strips red print; subcut strips into (96) 2½" N squares.
Step 10. Cut three 4½" by fabric width strips each cream floral (R) and green dot (O); subcut strips into (48) 2½" rectangles each fabric.

Step 11. Cut nine 2½" by fabric width strips green dot; subcut strips into (144) 2½" squares. Draw a diagonal line from corner to corner on the wrong side of 96 squares for Q; set aside remaining 48 squares for P.

Step 12. Cut four 2⅞" by fabric width strips each cream floral (S) and green dot (T); subcut strips into (48) 2⅞" squares each fabric. Cut each square in half on one diagonal to make 96 each S and T triangles.

Step 13. Cut three 2½" by fabric width strips cream floral; subcut strips into (48) 2½" U squares.

Step 14. Cut seven 2¼" by fabric width strips cream floral for binding.

Completing the Blocks

Step 1. Draw a diagonal line from corner to corner on the wrong side of each M and N square.

Step 2. Referring to Figure 1, sew M to each corner of L on the marked line. Trim seam to ¼"; press M to the right side to complete a center unit. Repeat for 12 center units.

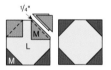

Figure 1

Step 3. Referring to Figure 2, sew N to O on the marked line; trim seam to ¼" and press N to the right side. Repeat with a second N on the remaining end of O to complete an N-O unit; repeat for 48 units.

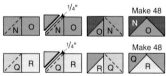

Figure 2   **Figure 3**

Step 4. Repeat Step 3 with Q and R pieces to complete 48 Q-R units, again referring to Figure 2.

Step 5. Sew S to T on the diagonal to complete an S-T unit; press seam toward T. Repeat for 96 S-T units.

Step 6. To complete one block, join one each Q-R and N-O units to make a side unit as shown in Figure 3; repeat for four side units. Press seams toward Q-R.

Step 7. Sew a side unit to opposite sides of the center unit as shown in Figure 4; press seams toward the center unit.

Figure 4

Step 8. Sew U to the T side of an S-T unit as shown in Figure 5; press seam toward U. Repeat for four S-T-U units.

Figure 5

Step 9. Sew P to the T side of an S-T unit, again referring to Figure 5; press seams toward P. Repeat for four P-S-T units.

Step 10. Join one S-T-U unit with one P-S-T unit to complete a corner unit as shown in Figure 6; press seams in one direction. Repeat for four corner units.

Figure 6

Step 11. Sew a corner unit to opposite sides of a side unit to make a row as shown in Figure 7; press seams toward corner units. Repeat for two rows.

Figure 7

Step 12. Sew a row to opposite sides of the center row to complete one block; press seams toward the center row. Repeat for 12 blocks.

Completing the Top

Step 1. Sew B to opposite sides of A and C to the top and bottom; press seams toward B and C.

Step 2. Sew D to opposite sides and E to the top and bottom of the bordered A square; press seams toward D and E.

Step 3. Join two blocks; press seams in one direction. Repeat for two two-block rows. Sew a row to the B-D sides of the bordered A square; press seams toward B.

Step 4. Join four blocks; press seams in one direction. Repeat for two four-block rows. Sew a row to the C-E sides of the bordered A square to complete the pieced center; press seams toward E.

Step 5. Sew F strips to opposite sides and G strips to the top and bottom of the pieced center; press seams toward F and G.

Step 6. Sew H strips to opposite sides and I strips to the top and bottom of the pieced center; press seams toward H and I.

Step 7. Sew J strips to opposite sides and K strips to the top and bottom of the pieced center; press seams toward J and K to complete the pieced top.

Step 8. Complete the quilt referring to Completing Your Quilt on page 175. ★

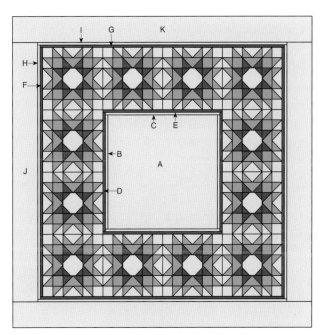

Grandmother's Stars
Placement Diagram
60" x 60"

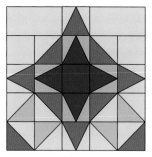

Side Ocean Star
12½" x 12½" Block
Make 4

Corner Ocean Star
12½" x 12½" Block
Make 4

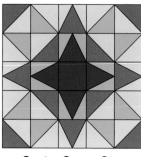

Center Ocean Star
12½" x 12½" Block
Make 1

DESIGN BY
CONNIE KAUFFMAN

Ocean Stars

The fabrics used in this pretty wall quilt create the feeling of a warm, tropical ocean.

Project Specifications

Skill Level: Beginner
Quilt Size: 37½" x 37½"
Block Size: 12½" x 12½"
Number of Blocks: 9

Fabric & Batting

All fabrics used are batik.
- ¼ yard aqua mottled
- ⅜ yard navy mottled
- ½ yard green mottled
- ⅔ yard green/blue leaf print
- 1½ yards pale aqua dot
- Backing 43" x 43"
- Batting 43" x 43"

Supplies & Tools

- All-purpose thread to match fabrics
- Quilting thread
- Basic sewing tools and supplies

Cutting

Step 1. Prepare templates for pieces B/G and C/H using patterns given. Cut two strips each navy mottled (B) and green/blue leaf print (G) 3" by fabric width. Cut 36 each B and G pieces from the strips as shown in Figure 1.

Figure 1

Step 2. Cut three strips each green mottled (C) and pale aqua dot (H) 3" by fabric width; fold each strip in half across width. Cut 36 each C and CR and H and HR pieces from the strips as shown in Figure 2.

Figure 2

Step 3. Cut one green/blue leaf print (K), five navy mottled (A) and 20 pale aqua dot (F) 3" x 3" squares.
Step 4. Cut three 3⅜" by fabric width strips green/blue leaf print; subcut strips into (26) 3⅜" squares. Cut each square in half on one diagonal to make 52 D triangles.
Step 5. Cut four 3⅜" by fabric width strips pale aqua

dot; subcut strips into (42) 3⅜" E squares. Cut each square in half on one diagonal to make 84 E triangles.

Step 6. Cut eight 3⅜" x 3⅜" squares each green (J) and aqua (L) mottleds. Cut each square in half on one diagonal to make 16 each J and L triangles.

Step 7. Cut two 5½" by fabric width strips pale aqua dot; subcut strips into (20) 3" I rectangles.

Step 8. Cut four 2¼" by fabric width strips pale aqua dot for binding.

Piecing the Units

Step 1. Sew C and CR to B to make a B-C unit as shown in Figure 3; press seams toward C and CR. Repeat for 36 B-C units. Repeat with H and HR and G to complete 36 G-H units, again referring to Figure 3; press seams toward H and HR.

Figure 3

Step 2. Sew D to E along the diagonal to make a D-E unit as shown in Figure 4; repeat for 52 D-E units. Press seams toward D.

Figure 4

Step 3. Sew E to J along the diagonal to make an E-J unit, again referring to Figure 4; repeat for 16 E-J units. Press seams toward J.

Step 4. Sew E to L along the diagonal to make an E-L unit, again referring to Figure 4; repeat for 16 E-L units. Press seams toward L.

Completing the Blocks

Step 1. To complete the blocks, arrange units with A, F, K and I pieces in five rows referring to Figures 5, 6 and 7 for each block; press seams in adjacent rows in opposite directions.

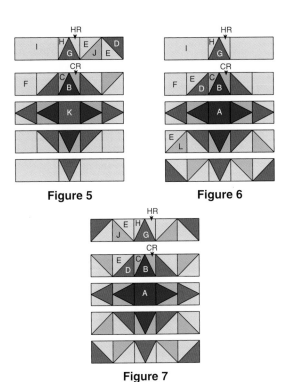

Figure 5   **Figure 6**

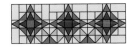

Figure 7

Ocean Stars
Placement Diagram
37½" x 37½"

Step 2. Join the rows to complete the blocks; press seams in one direction. Repeat to make one Center and four each Side and Corner Ocean Star blocks.

Completing the Top
Step 1. Join one Side and two Corner Ocean Star blocks to make a side row referring to Figure 8; repeat for two side rows. Press seams in one direction.

Figure 8

Step 2. Join the Center and two Side Ocean Star blocks to complete the center row referring to Figure 9; press seams in one direction.

Figure 9

Step 3. Join the center and side rows referring to the Placement Diagram for positioning of rows; press seams in one direction to complete the top.
Step 4. Complete the quilt referring to Completing Your Quilt on page 175. ★

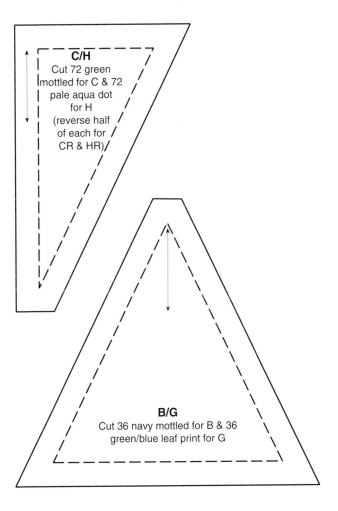

C/H
Cut 72 green mottled for C & 72 pale aqua dot for H (reverse half of each for CR & HR)

B/G
Cut 36 navy mottled for B & 36 green/blue leaf print for G

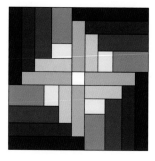

Shimmering Star
19" x 19" Block

DESIGN BY
CONNIE KAUFFMAN

Shimmering Stars

Half Log-Cabin units form a twist-and-turn star design over the top of this night-sky-color quilt.

Project Specifications

Skill Level: Beginner
Quilt Size: 78" x 105½"
Block Size: 19" x 19"
Number of Blocks: 15

Fabric & Batting

All blue fabrics used are tonals, mottleds or prints

- ⅛ yard white-with-blue print
- ⅝ yard lightest blue
- 1 yard medium/light blue
- 1¼ yards medium blue
- 1¼ yards light blue
- 1½ yards dark blue
- 1¾ yards dark/medium blue
- 2¼ yards darkest blue
- Backing 84" x 110"
- Batting 84" x 110"

Supplies & Tools

- All-purpose thread to match fabrics
- Quilting thread
- Basic sewing tools and supplies

Cutting

Step 1. Cut eight 5¼" by fabric width strips medium blue; subcut strips into (88) 3¼" A rectangles.

Step 2. Cut six 3¼" by fabric width strips lightest blue; subcut strips into (88) 2¾" B rectangles.

Step 3. Cut five 7½" by fabric width strips dark/medium blue; subcut strips into (88) 2¾" C strips.

Step 4. Cut five 5½" by fabric width strips light blue; subcut strips into (88) 2¼" D strips.

Step 5. Cut five 9¼" by fabric width strips dark blue; subcut strips into (88) 2¼" E strips.

Step 6. Cut five 7¼" by fabric width strips medium/light blue; subcut strips into (88) 2¼" F strips.

Step 7. Cut five 11" by fabric width strips darkest blue; subcut strips into (88) 2¼" G strips.

Step 8. Cut one 2½" by fabric width strip white-with-blue print; subcut strip into (15) 2½" H squares.

Step 9. Cut one 11" by fabric width strip light blue; subcut strip into (15) 2½" I strips.

Step 10. Cut (10) 2¼" by fabric width strips dark/medium blue for binding.

Completing the Blocks

Step 1. Sew B to the short side of A; press seam toward B.

Step 2. Add C to the A-B unit as shown in Figure 1; press seam toward C.

Figure 1

Figure 2

Figure 3

Step 3. Sew D to the B-C end of the A-B-C unit as shown in Figure 2; press seam toward D.

Step 4. Add E, F and then G to complete a block unit referring to Figure 3; press seams toward E, F and G. Repeat for 88 block units. Set aside 28 block units.

Step 5. To complete one block, sew a block unit to H with a partial seam as shown in Figure 4; press seam away from H.

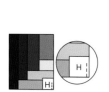
Figure 4

Figure 5

Figure 6

Step 6. Add a second block unit to the adjacent side of H as shown in Figure 5: press seams away from H.

Step 7. Add a third block unit to H; press seam away from H.

Step 8. Add a fourth block unit to H, folding the block unit away at the partial seam as shown in Figure 6; press seam away from H.

Step 9. Complete the partial seam to complete one block as shown in Figure 7; press seam away from H. Repeat for 15 blocks.

Figure 7

Figure 8

Figure 9

Completing the Top

Step 1. Sew an I strip to the long A side of a block unit as shown in Figure 8 to make an I unit; repeat for 15 I units. Press seams toward I.

Step 2. Join one block unit with one I unit to make a side unit as shown in Figure 9; repeat for 13 side units.

Step 3. Join three Shimmering Star blocks with two side units to complete a block row as shown in Figure 10; repeat for five block rows. Press seams in one direction.

Figure 10

Step 4. Join two I units with three side units to complete the top row as shown in Figure 11; press seams in one direction.

Figure 11

Step 5. Join the block rows and add the top row to complete the pieced top; press seams in one direction.

Step 6. Complete the quilt referring to Completing Your Quilt on page 175. ★

Shimmering Stars
Placement Diagram
78" x 105½"

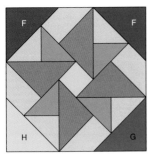

Island Sunrise A
9" x 9" Block
Make 4

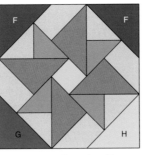

Island Sunrise B
9" x 9" Block
Make 4

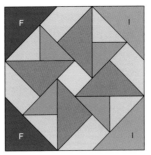

Island Sunrise C
9" x 9" Block
Make 2

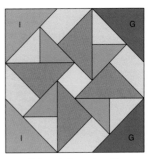

Island Sunrise D
9" x 9" Block
Make 2

DESIGN BY
LINDA MILLER

Island Sunrise

Try this unique method of preparing paper patterns to make this beautiful throw.

Project Specifications

Skill Level: Intermediate
Quilt Size: 54" x 63"
Block Size: 9" x 9" and 7" x 7"
Number of Blocks: 24

Fabric & Batting

All fabrics used are batiks.
- ¼ yard dark purple print
- ⅜ yard blue/violet mottled
- ½ yard magenta mottled
- ¾ yard blue/purple/tan print
- 1 yard peach multicolor mottled
- 1¼ yards purple/rust print
- 1¼ yards light blue mottled
- 2 yards multicolor fern print
- Backing 60" x 69"
- Batting 60" x 69"

Supplies & Tools

- All-purpose thread to match fabrics
- Quilting thread
- Tissue paper
- Basic sewing tools and supplies

Left Stripe
9" x 9" Block
Make 4

Right Stripe
9" x 9" Block
Make 4

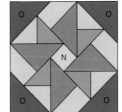

Island Sunrise Corner
7" x 7" Block
Make 4

Cutting

Step 1. Cut one 2⅛" by fabric width strip peach multicolor mottled; subcut strip into (12) 2⅛" A squares and four 1¾" x 1¾" N squares.

Step 2. Cut six 3½" by fabric width strips each

blue/purple/tan print (C) and light blue mottled (D); subcut strips into (64) 3½" squares each for C and D.

Step 3. Cut six 5¾" by fabric width strips purple/rust print; subcut strips into (64) 3½" B rectangles.

Step 4. Cut four 4¼" by fabric width strips light blue mottled; subcut strips into (64) 2½" E rectangles.

Step 5. Cut two 4¼" by fabric width strips each blue/violet (F) and magenta (G) mottleds; subcut strips into (12) 4¼" squares each fabric. Cut each square in half on one diagonal to make 24 each F and G triangles.

Step 6. Cut four 4¼" x 4¼" squares each peach multicolor mottled (H) and multicolor fern print (I); cut each square in half on one diagonal to make eight each H and I triangles.

Step 7. Cut eight 2⅛" x 9¼" rectangles each purple/rust (J) and dark purple (L) prints. Cut each end of

each strip at a 45-degree angle as shown in Figure 1 to make J and L pieces.

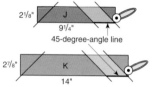

Figure 1

Step 8. Cut eight 2⅞" x 14" rectangles each multicolor fern print (K) and peach multicolor mottled (M). Cut each end of each rectangle at a 45-degree angle, again referring to Figure 1, to make K and M pieces.

Step 9. Cut eight 3½" x 3½" squares magenta mottled; cut each square in half on one diagonal to make 16 O triangles.

Step 10. Cut two 2½" x 36½" P strips peach multicolor mottled.

Step 11. Cut three 2½" by fabric width strips peach multicolor mottled. Join strips on short ends to make one long strip; press seams open. Subcut strips into two 49½" Q strips.

Step 12. Cut two 7½" x 40½" S strips and two 7½" x 49½" R strips along the length of the multicolor fern print.

Step 13. Cut five 2¼"-wide strips along the length of the remaining multicolor fern print for binding.

Completing the A–D & Corner Blocks

Step 1. Make paper copies of Foundation 1 and 2 as directed with patterns and stitch units using traditional paper-piecing methods referring to Basic Paper Piecing in the General Instructions on page 173, or refer to Precision With Tissue Paper on pages 150 and 151 for designer's special paper-piecing technique.

Step 2. Sew one Foundation 1 unit to A, stopping stitching ½" from edge of A as shown in Figure 2; press seam away from A.

Figure 2   **Figure 3**

Step 3. Pin and sew another Foundation 1 unit to the stitched unit on the end with the completed seam as shown in Figure 3; press seam away from A.

Step 4. Add another unit to A in this same fashion; complete the partially stitched seam of the first unit as shown in Figure 4 to complete a block center. Repeat for 12 block centers.

Figure 4

Step 5. Referring to the block drawings, add corner triangles to complete four each A and B blocks and two each C and D blocks.

Step 6. Repeat Steps 2–5 with Foundation 2 patterns, N squares and O triangles to create four corner blocks, again referring to the block drawing.

Completing the Left & Right Stripe Blocks

Step 1. To complete one Right Stripe block, sew J to K and add F to the J side as shown in Figure 5; press seams toward J and F.

Figure 5   **Figure 6**

Step 2. Sew L to M and add G to the L side as shown in Figure 6; press seams toward L and G.

Step 3. Join the F-J-K unit with the G-L-M unit to complete one Right Stripe block as shown in Figure 7; press seam toward K. Repeat for four Right Stripe blocks.

Figure 7

Step 4. Repeat Steps 1 and 2, substituting a second G triangle for F as shown in Figure 8.

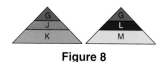

Figure 8

Step 5. Join the G-L-M unit with the G-J-K unit to complete one Left Stripe block referring to Figure 9; press seam toward M. Repeat for four Left Stripe blocks.

Figure 9

Completing the Top

Step 1. Join two A and two B blocks to make an X row as shown in Figure 10; press seams in one direction. Repeat for two rows.

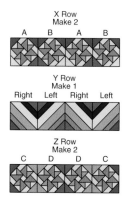

Figure 10

Island Sunrise
Placement Diagram
54" x 63"

Step 2. Join two Left Stripe and two Right Stripe blocks to make a Y row, again referring to Figure 10; press seams in one direction. Repeat for two rows.

Step 3. Join two C and two D blocks to make a Z row, again referring to Figure 10; press seams in one direction.

Step 4. Join the rows referring to the Placement Diagram for positioning; press seams in one direction.

Step 5. Sew a P strip to the top and bottom and Q strips to opposite long sides of the pieced center; press seams toward P and Q strips.

Step 6. Sew an R strip to opposite long sides of the pieced center; press seams toward R strips.

Step 7. Sew an Island Sunrise Corner block to each end of each S strip; press seams toward S strips. Sew these strips to the top and bottom of the pieced center to complete the pieced top; press seams toward S-block strips.

Step 8. Remove all paper foundations.

Step 9. Complete the quilt referring to Completing Your Quilt on page 175. ★

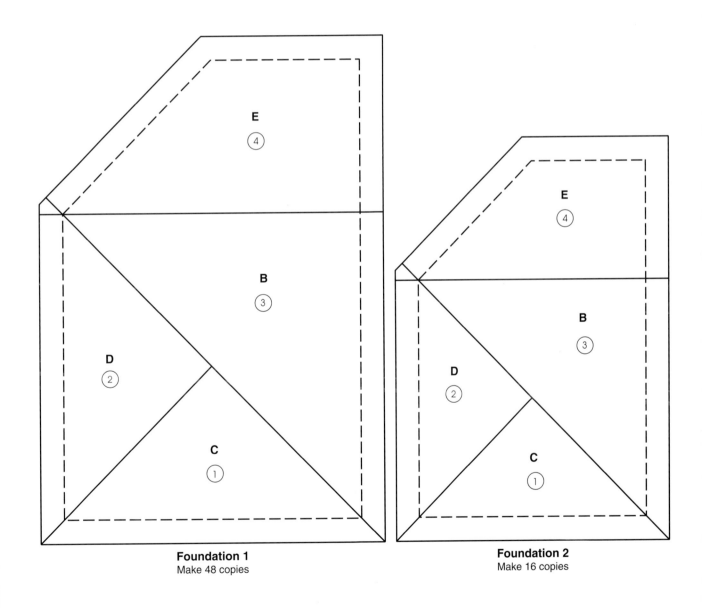

Foundation 1
Make 48 copies

Foundation 2
Make 16 copies

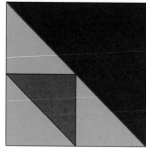
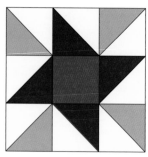

Welcome Home
6" x 6" Block
Make 13

Spinning Star
6" x 6" Block
Make 12

DESIGN BY
JILL REBER

Welcome Home

This quilt was made to honor the designer's
daughter-in-law on her safe return home from Iraq
where she served for one year. Her unit is called the
Eyes of Lightning and this insignia is stitched
on the label on the back of the quilt.

Project Specifications
Skill Level: Beginner
Quilt Size: 38" x 38"
Block Size: 6" x 6"
Number of Blocks: 25

Fabric & Batting
- ½ yard gold tonal
- ½ yard cream tonal
- ½ yard navy print
- ⅔ yard navy tonal
- ¾ yard red tonal
- Backing 44" x 44"
- Batting 44" x 44"

Supplies & Tools
- All-purpose thread to match fabrics
- Quilting thread
- Gold pearl cotton
- Basic sewing tools and supplies

Cutting
Step 1. Cut two 3⅞" by fabric width strips gold tonal;
subcut strips into (20) 3⅞" squares. Cut each square
on one diagonal to make 40 A triangles; discard
one triangle.

Step 2. Cut one 3⅞" by fabric width strip red tonal;
subcut strip into seven 3⅞" squares. Cut each square
on one diagonal to make 14 B triangles; discard
one triangle.

Step 3. Cut one 6⅞" by fabric width strip navy tonal;
subcut strip into six 6⅞" squares. Cut one more 6⅞"
x 6⅞" square navy tonal. Cut each square on one
diagonal to make 14 C triangles; discard one triangle.

Step 4. Cut one 2½" by fabric width strip red tonal;
subcut strip into (12) 2½" D squares.

line and press open to complete two F-G units, again referring to Figure 1. Repeat to complete 48 F-G units.

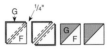

Figure 1

Step 2. Repeat Step 1 with E and F squares to complete 48 E-F units referring to Figure 2.

Figure 2

Step 3. To complete one Spinning Star block, sew an E-F unit to opposite sides of D to complete the center row as shown in Figure 3; press seams toward D.

Figure 3

Step 4. Join one E-F unit with two F-G units to complete a side row as shown in Figure 4; press seams toward F-G units. Repeat for two side rows.

Figure 4

Step 5. Sew a side row to opposite sides of the center row to complete one Spinning Star block referring to the block drawing; press seams in one direction. Repeat for 12 blocks.

Completing the Welcome Home Blocks

Step 1. Sew A to B on the diagonal; add an A to each remaining side of B as shown in Figure 5 to complete an A-B unit. Press seams toward A; repeat for 13 A-B units.

Figure 5

Step 5. Cut two 2⅞" by fabric width strips each navy (E) and gold (G) tonals; subcut strips into (24) 2⅞" squares each fabric.

Step 6. Cut four 2⅞" by fabric width strips cream tonal; subcut strips into (48) 2⅞" F squares. Draw a diagonal line from corner to corner on the wrong side of each F square.

Step 7. Cut two 1½" x 30½" H strips and two 1½" x 32½" I strips red tonal.

Step 8. Cut two 3½" x 32½" J strips and two 3½" x 38½" K strips navy print.

Step 9. Cut four 2¼" by fabric width strips red tonal for binding.

Completing the Spinning Star Blocks

Step 1. Place a G square right sides together with an F square; stitch ¼" on each side of the drawn line on F as shown in Figure 1; cut apart on the drawn

Step 2. Sew C to an A-B unit as shown in Figure 6 to complete one Welcome Home block; press seam toward D. Repeat for 13 blocks.

Figure 6

Completing the Top

Step 1. Join two Spinning Star blocks with three Welcome Home blocks to make an X row as shown in Figure 7; repeat for three X rows. Press seams toward Welcome Home blocks.

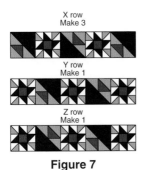

X row
Make 3

Y row
Make 1

Z row
Make 1

Figure 7

Step 2. Join two Welcome Home blocks with three Spinning Star blocks to make a Y row, again referring to Figure 7; press seams toward Welcome Home blocks.

Step 3. Join two Welcome Home blocks with three Spinning Star blocks to make a Z row, again referring to Figure 7; press seams toward Welcome Home blocks.

Step 4. Arrange rows and join referring to the Placement Diagram for positioning; press seams in one direction.

Step 5. Sew an H strip to opposite sides and I strips to the top and bottom of the pieced center; press seams toward H and I strips.

Step 6. Sew a J strip to opposite sides and K strips to the top and bottom of the pieced center; press seams toward J and K strips to complete the top.

Step 7. Complete the quilt referring to Completing Your Quilt on page 175, quilting the star design given in the C triangles using gold pearl cotton. ★

Star Quilting Design

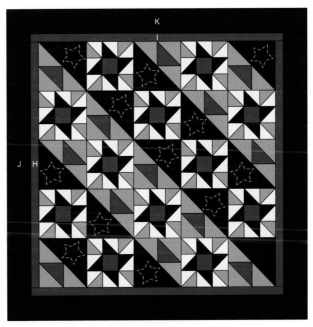

Welcome Home
Placement Diagram
38" x 38"

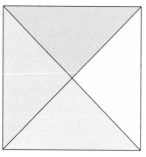

Triangles A
9" x 9" Block
Make 24

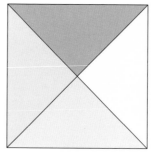

Triangles B
9" x 9" Block
Make 14

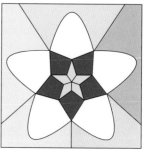

Ahoya Flower
9" x 9" Block
Make 14

DESIGN BY
DOLORES KEATON

Ahoya Flowers

Large pieced-and-appliquéd leaves adorn the borders of this interesting star-flower design.

Project Specifications

Skill Level: Advanced
Quilt Size: 69" x 87"
Block Size: 9" x 9"
Number of Blocks: 52

Fabric & Batting

- 1 fat quarter yellow mottled
- 8–10 fat quarters various light greens
- 8–10 fat quarters various dark greens
- ⅓ yard medium green mottled
- ⅜ yard yellow print
- ½ yard black-with-white check
- ⅔ yard red/black print
- 1 yard white tonal
- 1¾ yards black tonal
- 4½ yards total or 18–24 fat quarters white-with-black prints
- Backing 75" x 93"
- Batting 75" x 93"

Supplies & Tools

- All-purpose thread to match fabrics
- Quilting thread

- 1½ yards lightweight interfacing
- ⅜" bias bar
- Basic sewing tools and supplies

Cutting

Step 1. Prepare templates using pattern pieces given; cut as directed on each piece.

Step 2. Cut (35) 10¼" x 10¼" squares white-with-black prints; cut each square on both diagonals to make 140 I triangles. Discard two triangles.

Step 3. Cut four 10¼" x 10¼" squares black-with-white check; cut each square on both diagonals to make 16 J triangles. Discard two triangles.

Step 4. Cut four black tonal (K) and eight yellow print (L) rectangles 5" x 9½".

Step 5. Cut eight 1½" by fabric width strips red/black print. Join strips on short ends to make one long strip; subcut strip into two 73" M strips and two 91" N strips.

Step 6. Cut eight 2½" by fabric width strips black tonal. Join strips on short ends to make one long strip; subcut strip into two 73" O strips and two 91" P strips.

Step 7. Cut 1"-wide bias strips from medium green mottled and join to total 200".

Step 8. Enlarge leaf patterns 400 percent by photocopying or scanning or use graph given to create a pattern.

Step 9. Cut six interfacing patterns for each side of Leaf 1 and four for each side of Leaf 2.

Step 10. Cut a variety of strips from the light and dark green fat quarters in varying widths from 1"–2½".

Step 11. Cut eight 2¼" by fabric width strips black tonal for binding.

Completing the Ahoya Flower Blocks

Step 1. To complete one Ahoya Flower block, sew B to each side of A, stopping at the end of the marked seam allowance as shown in Figure 1; repeat for two A-B units. Press seams toward B.

Figure 1　　　**Figure 2**

Step 2. Join the two A-B units with one B and three A pieces to complete the block center as shown in Figure 2; press seams toward B.

Step 3. Set a Q piece between the B angles as shown in Figure 3; press seams toward B.

Figure 3

Step 4. Sew C between D and DR; press seams toward C. Sew E to ER; press seam toward ER. Join

the two units to complete a block background as shown in Figure 4; press seams toward D and DR.

Figure 4

Step 5. Arrange the A-B-Q unit on the block background, matching seams of the block background with seams on the A-B-Q unit referring to the block drawing; baste in place.

Step 6. Hand-stitch the A-B-Q unit in place, turning under the edges of Q as you stitch to complete one Ahoya Flower block; repeat for 14 blocks.

Completing the Triangle Blocks

Step 1. Join two I triangles as shown in Figure 5; press seams in one direction. Repeat for two I units.

Figure 5　　　**Figure 6**　　　**Figure 7**

Step 2. Join the two I units to complete one Triangles A block as shown in Figure 6; press seam in one direction. Repeat for 24 blocks.

Step 3. Sew I to J as shown in Figure 7; press seam toward J.

Step 4. Join two I triangles as in Step 1.

Step 5. Join the I-J unit with the I unit to complete one Triangles B block as shown in Figure 8; press seam in one direction. Repeat for 14 blocks.

Figure 8　　　**Figure 9**

Completing the Leaves

Step 1. Place one light green strip angled in the center of one Leaf 1 light-side interfacing piece referring to the line on the leaf pattern; pin a second strip right sides together with the first strip and stitch as shown in Figure 9.

Step 2. Press the second strip to the right side. Continue adding strips on both sides of the center strip until the entire interfacing leaf is covered as

shown in Figure 10; trim edges of strips ¼" larger all around the interfacing leaf pattern to complete one Leaf 1 half. Repeat for six of each half for Leaf 1 and four of each half for Leaf 2.

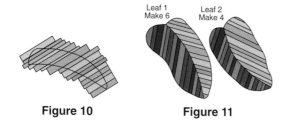

Leaf 1
Make 6

Leaf 2
Make 4

Figure 10   **Figure 11**

Step 3. Join leaf halves to complete six Leaf 1 and four Leaf 2 leaves as shown in Figure 11.

Completing the Top

Step 1. Sew a white tonal F to a black tonal F to complete an F unit as shown in Figure 12; press seam toward black tonal F. Repeat for four F and four FR units, again referring to Figure 12.

Make 4   Make 4

F
F

FR
FR

G   H

H
G
H

Figure 12   **Figure 13**   **Figure 14**

Step 2. Sew H to G as shown in Figure 13; repeat for two H-G units. Press seams toward H.

Step 3. Join two H-G units to complete a side unit as shown in Figure 14; repeat for two side units.

Step 4. Join two each K and L pieces and two Ahoya Flower blocks with one each F and FR unit to make a row as shown in Figure 15; press seams in one direction. Repeat for two rows.

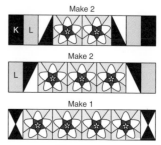

Make 2

K L

Make 2

L

Make 1

Figure 15

Step 5. Join two L pieces, one each F and FR unit and three Ahoya Flower blocks to make a row, again referring to Figure 15; press seams in the opposite direction from the previous rows. Repeat for two rows.

Step 6. Join two G-H units with four Ahoya Flower blocks to make the center row, again referring to Figure 15; press seams in one direction.

Step 7. Join the rows referring to the Placement Diagram for positioning; press seams in one direction.

Step 8. Join five Triangle A blocks to make a side row; press seams in one direction. Repeat for two side rows.

Step 9. Sew a side row to opposite sides of the pieced center; press seams toward side rows.

Step 10. Join seven Triangle A blocks to make a top row; press seams in one direction. Repeat for a bottom row.

Step 11. Sew the top and bottom rows to the pieced center; press seams toward top and bottom rows.

Step 12. Join seven Triangle B blocks as shown in Figure 16 to make a row; press seams in one direction. Repeat for two rows. Sew the rows to the top and bottom of the pieced center with the J triangles toward the outside edge referring to the Placement Diagram; press seams toward rows.

Figure 16

Step 13. Sew an M strip to an O strip with right sides together along length; press seams toward M. Repeat for two M-O strips. Repeat with N and P strips to make two N-P strips.

Step 14. Center and sew an M-O strip to the top and bottom and N-P strips to opposite sides of the pieced center, mitering corners. Trim corner seams to ¼" at mitered seam; press seams open as shown in Figure 17. Press border seams toward borders.

Figure 17

Step 15. Cut bias strip into the following lengths: one 6" (R), one 13" (S), five 10" (T), two 12¾" (U), one 16½" (V), one 38½" (W), one 12" (X) and one 4¾" (Y).

Step 16. Fold each cut bias strip in half along length with wrong sides together; stitch a ⅛" seam. Insert the ⅜"-wide bias bar inside the stitched strips, centering seam on one side; press.

Step 17. Referring to Figure 18, arrange strips on the pieced top. When satisfied with placement, hand-stitch in place, opening seams at block edges to tuck ends under as necessary. Re-stitch opened seams.

Figure 18

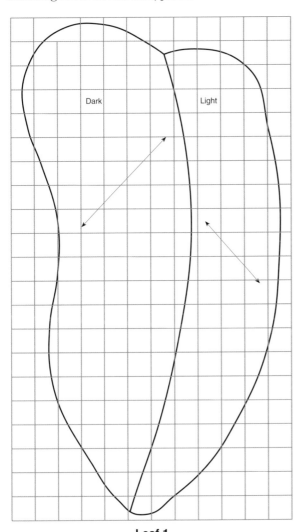

Leaf 1
1 square = 1"

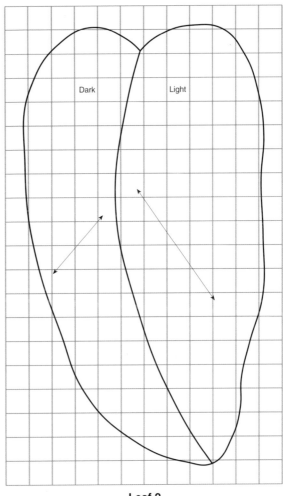

Leaf 2
1 square = 1"

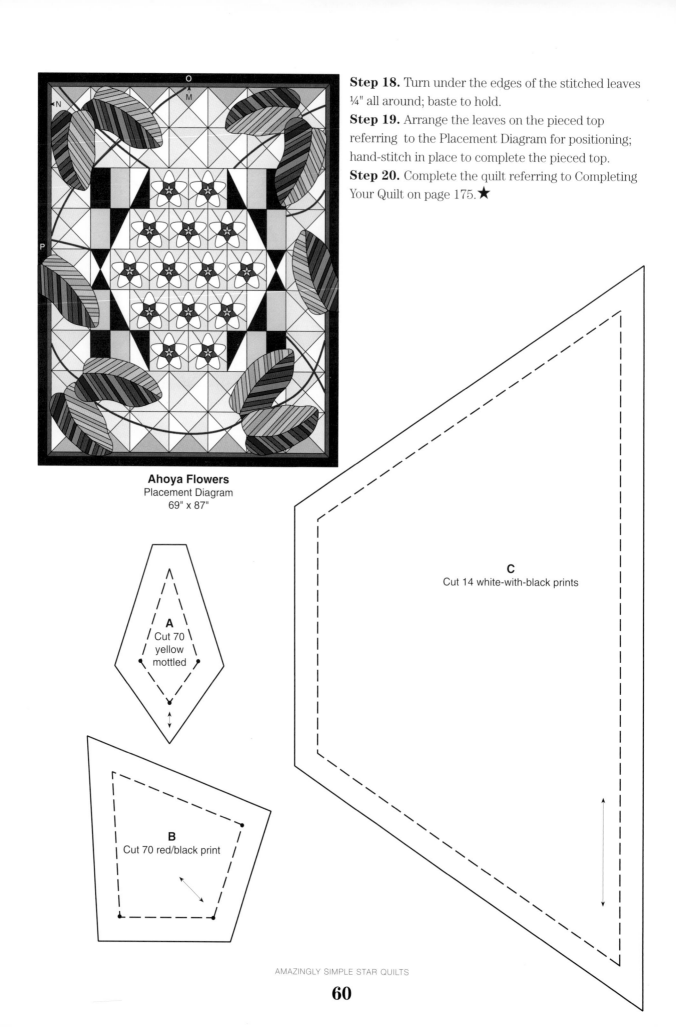

Ahoya Flowers
Placement Diagram
69" x 87"

Step 18. Turn under the edges of the stitched leaves ¼" all around; baste to hold.
Step 19. Arrange the leaves on the pieced top referring to the Placement Diagram for positioning; hand-stitch in place to complete the pieced top.
Step 20. Complete the quilt referring to Completing Your Quilt on page 175.★

A
Cut 70
yellow
mottled

B
Cut 70 red/black print

C
Cut 14 white-with-black prints

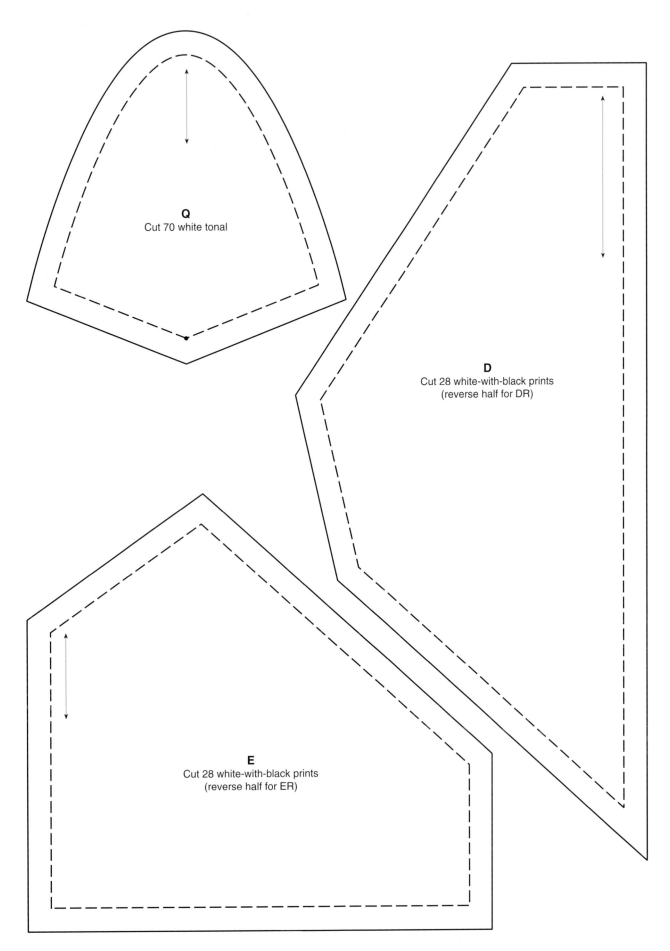

Q
Cut 70 white tonal

D
Cut 28 white-with-black prints
(reverse half for DR)

E
Cut 28 white-with-black prints
(reverse half for ER)

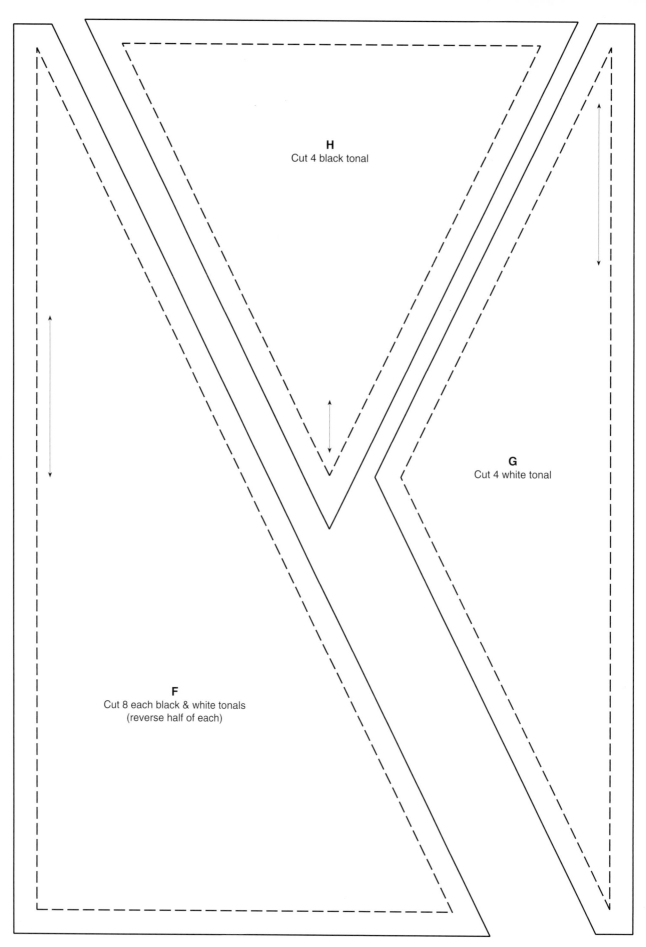

H
Cut 4 black tonal

G
Cut 4 white tonal

F
Cut 8 each black & white tonals
(reverse half of each)

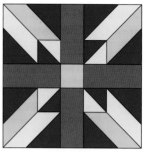

Shining Star
12" x 12" Block

DESIGN BY
CONNIE RAND

Shining Stars

Sparkly yellow and gold fabrics make these stars shine.

Project Specifications

Skill Level: Intermediate
Quilt Size: 64" x 76"
Block Size: 12" x 12"
Number of Blocks: 20

Materials

- 1 yard gold sparkle
- 1⅛ yards yellow sparkle
- 2 yards red print
- 2½ yards dark blue mottled
- Backing 70" x 82"
- Batting 70" x 82"

Supplies & Tools

- All-purpose thread to match fabrics
- Quilting thread
- Basic sewing tools and supplies

Cutting

Step 1. Cut three 2⅞" by fabric width strips dark blue mottled; subcut strips into (40) 2⅞" squares. Cut each square on one diagonal to make 80 A triangles.

Step 2. Cut three 2⅞" by fabric width strips yellow sparkle; subcut strips into (40) 2⅞" squares. Cut each square on one diagonal to make 80 B triangles.

Step 3. Cut eight 3⅞" by fabric width strips dark blue mottled; subcut strips into (80) 3⅞" squares. Cut each square on one diagonal to make 160 D triangles.

Step 4. Cut six 5½" by fabric width strips red print; set aside three strips for E. Cut the remaining strips into (40) 2½" G segments.

Step 5. Cut two 2½" by fabric width strips gold sparkle for F.

Step 6. Cut six 2½" by fabric width strips red print. Join strips on short ends to make one long strip; press seams open. Subcut strip into two 48½" H strips and two 64½" I strips.

Step 7. Cut seven 6½" by fabric width strips dark blue mottled. Join strips on short ends to make one long strip; press seams open. Subcut strip into two 52½" J strips and two 76½" K strips.

Step 8. Cut seven 2¼" by fabric width strips red print for binding.

Step 9. Prepare template for C; cut as directed on pattern.

Completing the Shining Star Blocks

Step 1. Sew an F strip between two E strips with right sides together along length. Cut the remaining E strip in half; sew the remaining F strip between the two half-E strips. Press seams toward E. Subcut strip sets into (20) 2½" segments for E-F units as shown in Figure 1.

Figure 1

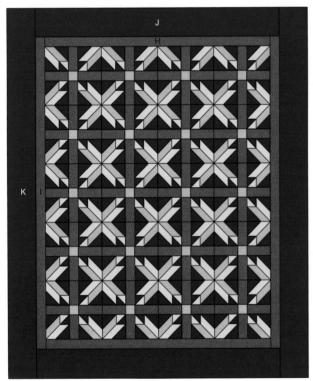

Shining Stars
Placement Diagram
64" x 76"

Step 2. To piece one block, sew A to CR and B to C and add D to each unit as shown in Figure 2; press seams toward B, CR and D. Repeat for four of each unit.

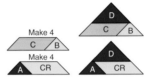

Figure 2   **Figure 3**

Step 3. Join two units to make a corner unit as shown in Figure 3; press seams toward gold sparkle unit. Repeat for four corner units.

Step 4. Join two corner units with G to make a side unit as shown in Figure 4; press seams toward G. Repeat for two side units.

Figure 4

Step 5. Sew an E-F strip between two side units as shown in Figure 5 to complete one Shining Star block; press seams toward the E-F unit. Repeat for 20 blocks.

Figure 5

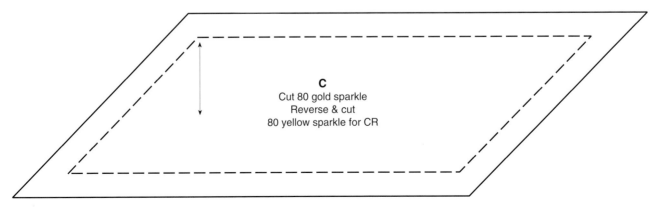

C
Cut 80 gold sparkle
Reverse & cut
80 yellow sparkle for CR

Completing the Quilt

Step 1. Join blocks in five rows of four blocks each as shown in Figure 6; press seams in one direction.

Figure 6

Step 2. Join block rows referring to the Placement Diagram to complete the pieced center; press seams in one direction.

Step 3. Add H strips to the top and bottom and I strips to opposite long sides of the pieced center; press seams toward H and I.

Step 4. Sew J strips to the top and bottom and K strips to opposite long sides of the pieced center to complete the pieced top; press seams toward J and K strips.

Step 5. Complete the quilt referring to Completing Your Quilt on page 175. ★

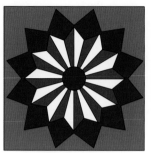

Spinning Star
10" x 10" Block
Make 10

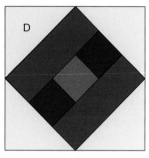

Garter
10" x 10" Block
Make 10

DESIGN BY
LINDA MILLER

Fireworks Fancy

Use paper piecing with appliqué to make this
patriotic star-design lap quilt.

Project Specifications
Skill Level: Intermediate
Quilt Size: 56" x 66"
Block Size: 10" x 10"
Number of Blocks: 20

Fabric & Batting
- ⅝ yard cream print
- ⅞ yard cream tonal
- 1⅛ yards red check
- 1¼ yards red print
- 1⅝ yards cream floral
- 1¾ yards blue print
- Backing 62" x 72"
- Batting 62" x 72"

Supplies & Tools
- All-purpose thread to match fabrics
- Quilting thread
- 4 yards fusible web
- Fabric glue stick
- Basic sewing tools and supplies

Cutting
Step 1. Make 40 copies of the Star Paper-Piecing
Pattern given. ***Note:*** *See designer's instructions
for making paper-piecing patterns on pages 150
and 151 or the General Instructions for Paper
Piecing on page 173.*
Step 2. Cut one 2⅞" by fabric width A strip
red check.
Step 3. Cut two 2⅞" by fabric width B strips
blue print.
Step 4. Cut four 2⅞" by fabric width strips red print;
subcut strips into (20) 7⅝" C rectangles.
Step 5. Cut three 5⅞" by fabric width strips cream
print; subcut strips into (20) 5⅞" squares. Cut each
square on one diagonal to make 40 D triangles.
Step 6. Cut six 4½" by fabric width strips each
cream tonal (E) and red print (F); subcut strips into
(120) 2" rectangles each for E and F.
Step 7. Cut (10) 10½" x 10½" I squares red check.
Fold and crease each square to mark the vertical,
horizontal and diagonal centers.
Step 8. Cut two 2½" x 40½" J strips blue print.
Step 9. Cut three 2½" by fabric width strips blue

print; join strips on short ends to make one long strip. Subcut strip into two 54½" K strips.

Step 10. Cut two 6½" x 54½" L strips and two 6½" x 56½" M strips along the length of the cream floral.

Step 11. Cut seven 2¼" by fabric width strips blue print for binding.

Step 12. Bond fusible web to the wrong side of the remaining blue print; trace and cut H circles and G star points as directed on patterns for number to cut. Remove paper backing after cutting all pieces.

Completing the Spinning Star Blocks

Step 1. Using the E and F rectangles with the Star Paper-Piecing patterns, and referring to the General Instructions for Paper Piecing on page 173 or the designer's method on pages 150 and 151, complete 40 E-F star units as shown in Figure 1.

Figure 1   **Figure 2**

Step 2. Join two E-F units to complete half the star design as shown in Figure 2; press seams open. Repeat for two half units. Join the half units to complete a star shape.

Step 3. Center the star shape on an I square as shown in Figure 3 and secure in place with the fabric glue stick.

Figure 3   **Figure 4**

Step 4. Carefully place a G star point on the edges of the star shape, overlapping star shape approximately ⅛" and aligning points as shown in Figure 4; fuse in place. Repeat with second G star point on the other half of the star shape, butting ends of G where they meet.

Step 5. Center the H circle over the center of the star shape; fuse in place.

Step 6. Stitch G and H pieces in place using a machine buttonhole stitch and cream thread to complete one Spinning Star block; repeat for 10 blocks.

Completing the Garter Blocks

Step 1. Sew a B strip to each side of an A strip with right sides together along length; press seams toward B. Subcut strip set into (10) 2⅞" A-B segments as shown in Figure 5.

Figure 5   **Figure 6**

Step 2. Sew C to each side of an A-B segment to make an A-B-C unit as shown in Figure 6; press seams toward C.

Step 3. Sew a D triangle to each side of the A-B-C unit to complete one Garter block; press seams toward D. Repeat for 10 blocks.

Completing the Top

Step 1. Join two Spinning Star blocks with two Garter blocks to make a row as shown in Figure 7; repeat for five rows. Press seams toward Garter blocks.

Make 5

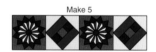

Figure 7

Fireworks Fancy
Placement Diagram
56" x 66"

Step 2. Join the rows referring to the Placement Diagram to complete the pieced center; press seams in one direction.

Step 3. Sew J strips to the top and bottom and K strips to opposite long sides of the pieced center; press seams toward J and K strips.

Step 4. Sew L to opposite long sides and M to the top and bottom of the pieced center; press seams toward L and M strips to complete the top.

Step 5. Complete the quilt referring to Completing Your Quilt on page 175. ★

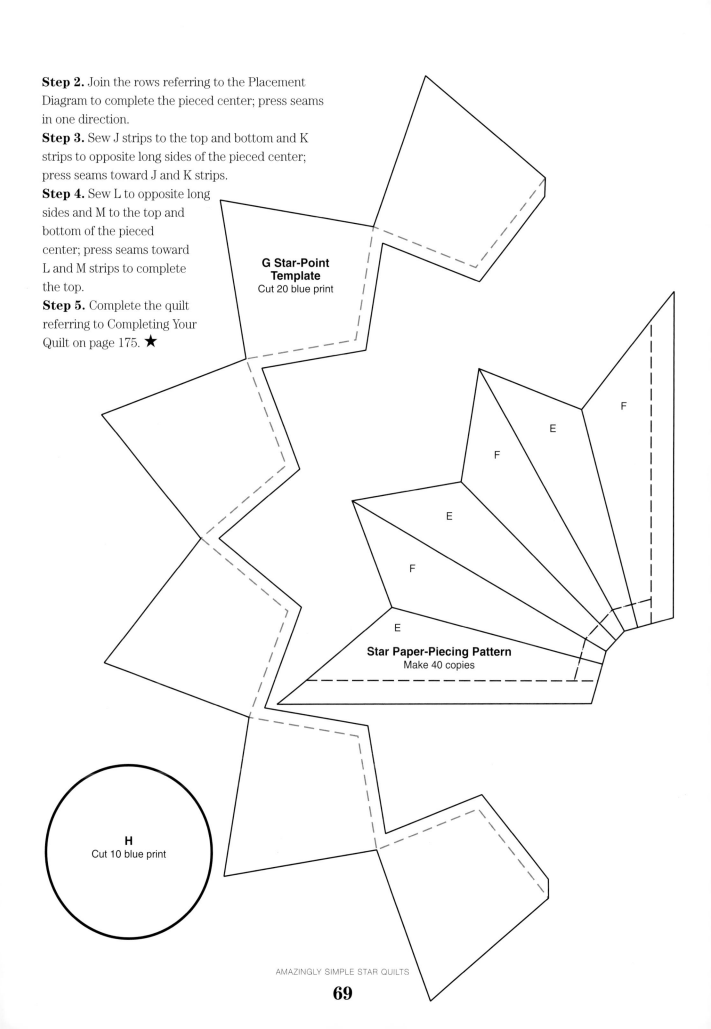

G Star-Point Template
Cut 20 blue print

F

E

F

F

E

F

E

Star Paper-Piecing Pattern
Make 40 copies

H
Cut 10 blue print

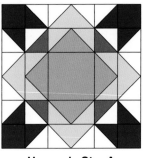

Heavenly Star A
18" x 18" Block
Make 10

Heavenly Star B
18" x 18" Block
Make 10

DESIGN BY
JUDITH SANDSTROM

Heavenly Stars

The blocks' corners meet to form a star design in this simple quilt made with triangles and squares.

Project Specifications
Skill Level: Beginner
Quilt Size: 72" x 90"
Block Size: 18" x 18"
Number of Blocks: 20

Fabric & Batting
- ⅞ yard mauve tonal
- 1⅝ yards dark mauve tonal
- 1⅞ yards navy print
- 2⅛ yards light blue print
- 2⅛ yards white tonal
- Backing 78" x 96"
- Batting 78" x 96"

Supplies & Tools
- All-purpose thread to match fabrics
- Quilting thread
- Basic sewing tools and supplies

Cutting
Step 1. Cut two 6½" by fabric width strips each navy print (A) and mauve tonal (I); subcut strips into (10) 6½" squares each for A and I.

Step 2. Cut four 7¼" by fabric width strips light blue print; subcut strips into (20) 7¼" squares. Cut each square in half on both diagonals to make 80 B triangles.

Step 3. Cut six 3⅞" by fabric width strips dark mauve tonal; subcut strips into (60) 3⅞" squares. Cut each square in half on one diagonal to make 120 C triangles.

Step 4. Repeat Step 3 with eight 3⅞" by fabric width strips light blue print to cut (80) 3⅞" squares and 160 F triangles.

Step 5. Cut four 3½" by fabric width strips each dark mauve tonal (D), light blue print (G) and navy print (L); subcut strips into (40) 3½" squares each color.

Step 6. Repeat Step 3 with (18) 3⅞" by fabric width strips white tonal to cut (180) 3⅞" squares and 360 E triangles.

Step 7. Repeat Step 2 with two 7¼" by fabric width strips each mauve (J) and dark mauve (H) tonals to cut (10) 7¼" squares each fabric and 40 each H and J triangles.

Step 8. Repeat Step 3 with four 3⅞" by fabric width strips navy print to cut (40) 3⅞" squares and 80 K triangles.

Step 9. Cut eight 2¼" by fabric width strips navy print for binding.

Completing the A Blocks

Step 1. Sew F to two short sides of J as shown in Figure 1; press seams toward F. Repeat for 40 F-J units. Repeat with E on two short sides of B to make 40 B-E units, again referring to Figure 1; press seams toward E.

Figure 1

Step 2. Join an F-J unit with a B-E unit to complete a side unit as shown in Figure 2; repeat for 40 side units. Press seams toward F-J units.

Figure 2

Step 3. Sew C to E along the diagonal to make a C-E unit as shown in Figure 3; repeat for 40 C-E units. Repeat with E and K to make 80 E-K units, again referring to Figure 3; press seams toward K.

Figure 3

Step 4. Join one C-E unit with two E-K units and one L square as shown in Figure 4 to complete a corner unit; press seams toward K and L and the E-K-L unit. Repeat for 40 corner units.

Figure 4

Step 5. To complete one A block, sew a side unit to opposite sides of I as shown in Figure 5 to complete the center row; press seams toward I.

Figure 5   **Figure 6**

Step 6. Sew a corner unit to opposite sides of a side unit as shown in Figure 6 to complete a side row; press seams toward corner units. Repeat for two side rows.

Step 7. Sew the side rows to opposite sides of the center row as shown in Figure 7 to complete one A block; press seams toward side rows. Repeat for 10 A blocks.

Figure 7

Completing the B Blocks

Step 1. Sew C to two short sides of B as shown in Figure 1; press seams toward C. Repeat for 40 B-C units. Repeat with E on two short sides of H to make 40 E-H units, again referring to Figure 1; press seams toward E.

Step 2. Join a B-C unit with an E-H unit to complete a side unit as shown in Figure 2; repeat for 40 side units. Press seams toward B-C units.

Step 3. Sew E to F along the diagonal to make an E-F unit as shown in Figure 3; repeat for 80 E-F units. Press seams toward F.

Step 4. Join one D and one G with two E-F units as shown in Figure 8 to complete a corner unit; press seams toward D and G and the E-F-G unit. Repeat for 40 corner units.

Figure 8

Figure 9

Step 5. To complete one B block, sew a side unit to opposite sides of A as shown in Figure 9 to complete the center row; press seams toward A.

Step 6. Sew a corner unit to opposite sides of a side unit as shown in Figure 10 to complete a side row; press seams toward side units. Repeat for two side rows.

Figure 10

Step 7. Sew the side rows to opposite sides of the center row as shown in Figure 11 to complete one B

block; press seams toward center row. Repeat for 10 B blocks.

Figure 11

Completing the Top

Step 1. Join two B blocks with two A blocks to complete a block row as shown in Figure 12; repeat for five block rows. Press seams toward B blocks.

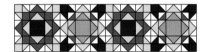

Figure 12

Step 2. Join the rows to complete the pieced top referring to the Placement Diagram for positioning of rows; press seams in one direction to complete the top.

Step 3. Complete the quilt referring to Completing Your Quilt on page 175. ★

Heavenly Stars
Placement Diagram
72" x 90"

Corner
8" x 8" Block
Make 4

True Colors
16" x 16" Block
Make 4

DESIGN BY
JULIE WEAVER

True Colors

This star-within-a-star design is made with the true patriotic colors of red, white and blue.

Project Specifications

Skill Level: Intermediate
Quilt Size: 48" x 48"
Block Size: 16" x 16" and 8" x 8"
Number of Blocks: 8

Fabric & Batting

- ¼ yard white print
- ⅓ yard red print
- ⅓ yard total assorted red scraps
- 1¼ yards navy print
- 1¼ yards total assorted white/cream scraps
- 1½ yards total assorted blue/navy scraps
- Backing 54" x 54"
- Batting 54" x 54"

Supplies & Tools

- All-purpose thread to match fabrics
- Quilting thread
- Basic sewing tools and supplies

Cutting

Step 1. Cut (24) 2½" x 2½" A squares from assorted red scraps.

Step 2. Cut (96) 1½" x 2½" B rectangles, (96) 1½" x 1½" D squares, (32) 2½" x 2½" G squares, (32) 2½" x 4½" E rectangles and (16) 4½" x 8½" H rectangles assorted blue/navy scraps.

Step 3. Cut (192) 1½" x 1½" C squares, (64) 2½" x 2½" F squares and (32) 4½" x 4½" I squares assorted white/cream scraps.

Step 4. Cut four 1¾" x 32½" J strips red print.

Step 5. Cut four 1¼" x 32½" K strips white print.

Step 6. Cut four 6½" x 32½" L strips navy print.

Step 7. Cut five 2¼" by fabric width strips navy print for binding.

Completing the Corner Blocks

Step 1. Draw a line from corner to corner on the wrong side of each C, F and I square.

Step 2. Referring to Figure 1 to complete a B-C unit, place a C square right sides together on one end of B; stitch on the marked line. Trim seam to ¼"; press C to the right side. Repeat on the opposite end of B to

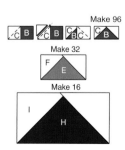

Make 96

Make 32

Make 16

Figure 1

complete a B-C unit. Repeat for 96 B-C units.

Step 3. Sew a B-C unit to opposite sides of A as shown in Figure 2; press seams toward A. Repeat for 24 A-B-C units.

Step 5. Sew a B-C-D unit to opposite sides of the A-B-C unit to complete a star unit referring to Figure 4; press seams toward B-C-D units. Repeat for 24 star units.

Figure 2

D

Figure 3

Step 4. Sew D to opposite ends of a B-C unit as shown in Figure 3; repeat for two units. Press seams toward D. Repeat for 48 B-C-D units.

Figure 4

Step 6. Repeat Step 2 with F and E to complete 32 E-F side units referring to Figure 1.

Step 7. To complete one Corner block, sew a side unit to opposite sides of a star unit as shown in Figure 5 to complete the center row; press seams toward side units.

Figure 5

Step 8. Sew G to each end of two E-F side units to complete the side rows referring to Figure 6; press seams toward side units.

Figure 6

Step 9. Sew a side row to opposite sides of the center row to complete one Corner block; repeat for four Corner blocks and four True Colors block centers referring to the Corner block drawing for positioning of rows. Press seams away from the center row.

Completing the True Colors Blocks

Step 1. Repeat Step 2 for Completing Corner blocks to complete 16 H-I units referring to Figure 1.

Step 2. To complete one True Colors block, sew an H-I unit to opposite sides of a True Colors block center as shown in Figure 7 to make the center row; press seams toward the H-I units.

Figure 7

Step 3. Sew a previously pieced small star unit to each end of each remaining H-I unit to complete the side rows as shown in Figure 8; press seams toward H-I units.

Figure 8

Step 4. Sew a side row to opposite sides of the center row to complete one True Colors block

referring to the block drawing for positioning; referring to Figure 8; press seams away from center row. Repeat for four blocks.

Completing the Top

Step 1. Join two True Colors blocks to make a row; repeat for two rows. Press seams in one direction.

Step 2. Join the two rows with seams in opposite directions to complete the pieced center; press seam in one direction.

Step 3. Sew a J strip to a K strip to an L strip with right sides together along the length to make a border strip; press seams away from K. Repeat to make four border strips.

Step 4. Sew a border strip to opposite sides of the pieced center; press seams toward border strips.

Step 5. Sew a Corner block to each end of each remaining border strip; press seams toward border strips. Sew these strips to the remaining sides of the pieced center to complete the top; press seams toward border strips.

Step 6. Complete the quilt referring to Completing Your Quilt on page 175. ★

True Colors
Placement Diagram
48" x 48"

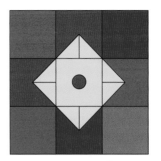

Prairie Points Star
9" x 9" Block

DESIGN BY
CHRIS MALONE

Prairie Points Throw

Star points are formed by the 3-D prairie points stitched around the edges of the yellow squares.

Project Notes

The sample uses 10 assorted yellow prints or tonals for making the star units, making three complete stars from each fabric. The red background squares are cut from a wide assortment of fabrics for a scrappy look. Thirty squares may be cut from a fat quarter.

Project Specifications

Skill Level: Beginner
Quilt Size: 45" x 54"
Block Size: 9" x 9"
Number of Blocks: 30

Fabric & Batting

- ½ yard red mottled for binding
- 1½ yards total yellow tonals or prints
- 2¼ yards total red tonals, prints or mottleds
- Backing 51" x 60"
- Batting 51" x 60"

Supplies & Tools

- All-purpose thread to match fabrics
- Quilting thread
- 30 assorted red ⅞" buttons
- Spray starch
- Basic sewing tools and supplies

Cutting

Step 1. Cut five matching 3½" x 3½" yellow A squares; repeat to cut 30 sets (150 squares total).
Step 2. Cut (240) 3½" x 3½" red B squares.
Step 3. Cut five 2¼" by fabric width strips red mottled for binding.

Completing the Star Units

Step 1. Fold an A square in half with wrong sides together; press. Find the center of the folded edge and make two diagonal folds down from this point, creating a triangle with a vertical fold in the center to complete a prairie point as shown in Figure 1; press. Spray with spray starch; press again. Repeat for four matching prairie points.

Figure 1

Step 2. Pin one folded prairie point with vertical fold against the right side of a matching A square and raw edges even; baste ⅛" from raw edge to hold in place. Repeat with the remaining prairie points as shown in Figure 2 to complete a star unit.

Figure 2

Step 3. Repeat Steps 1 and 2 to complete 30 star units.

Completing the Prairie Points Star Blocks

Step 1. To complete one block, sew a B square to the right and left side of a star unit as shown in Figure 3; press seams open to reduce bulk. Press side prairie points toward B.

Figure 3

Step 2. Join three B squares to complete one row; repeat for two rows. Press seams open.

Step 3. Join the rows to complete one block as shown in Figure 4; press seams open and prairie points toward B. Repeat for 30 blocks.

Figure 4

Completing the Top

Step 1. Join five blocks to make a row; repeat for six rows. Press seams in one direction.
Step 2. Join the rows to complete the quilt top.
Step 3. Complete the quilt referring to Completing Your Quilt on page 175.
Step 4. Sew a red button to the center of each A square of each block to complete the quilt. ★

Prairie Points Star Throw
Placement Diagram
45" x 54"

Green Star
20" x 20" Block
Make 6

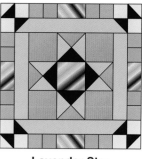

Lavender Star
20" x 20" Block
Make 6

DESIGN BY
SANDRA L. HATCH

Stars in the Crossroads

Bright florals create the pattern of stars
in the blocks and at the sashing corners.

Project Specifications

Skill Level: Beginner
Quilt Size: 86" x 109"
Block Size: 20" x 20"
Number of Blocks: 12

Fabric & Batting

- ½ yard green mottled
- ½ yard lavender tonal
- ⅔ yard lavender floral
- ⅔ yard green leaf tonal
- ¾ yard yellow mottled
- 2⅝ yards pink tonal
- 2⅝ yards large floral
- 3¼ yards purple tonal
- Backing 92" x 115"
- Batting 92" x 115"

Supplies & Tools

- Neutral color all-purpose thread
- Quilting thread
- Basic sewing tools and supplies

Cutting

Step 1. Cut two 4½" by fabric width strips large floral; subcut strips into (12) 4½" A squares.

Step 2. Cut two 5¼" by fabric width strips purple tonal; subcut strips into (12) 5¼" squares. Cut each square on both diagonals to make 48 B triangles.

Step 3. Cut one 5¼" by fabric width strip each green leaf tonal (D) and lavender floral (H); subcut strips into six 5¼" squares each fabric. Cut each square on both diagonals to make 24 each D and H triangles.

Step 4. Cut three 5¼" by fabric width strips pink tonal; subcut strips into (24) 5¼" squares. Cut each square on both diagonals to make 96 C triangles.

Step 5. Cut three 4½" by fabric width strips each green leaf tonal (E) and lavender floral (I); subcut

strips into (24) 4½" squares each for I and E.

Step 6. Cut two 12½" by fabric width strips pink tonal; subcut strips into (24) 2½" F strips.

Step 7. Cut two 16½" by fabric width strips pink tonal; subcut strips into (24) 2½" G strips. Subcut remainder of strips into eight 2½" x 12½" F strips.

Step 8. Cut three 4½" by fabric width J strips large floral; subcut strips into (48) 2½" J rectangles.

Step 9. Cut six 2½" by fabric width strips each yellow (K) and green mottleds (L) and lavender tonal (M).

Step 10. Cut three 2½" by fabric width strips purple tonal; subcut strips into (48) 2½" N squares. Draw a diagonal line from corner to corner on the wrong side of each square.

Step 11. Cut two 2⅞" by fabric width strips each yellow mottled (O) and purple tonal (P); subcut strips into (24) 2⅞" squares each fabric. Cut each square on one diagonal to make 48 each O and P triangles.

Step 12. Cut two 3½" by fabric width strips large floral; subcut strips into (20) 3½" Q squares.

Step 13. Cut three 20½" by fabric width strips purple tonal; subcut strips into (31) 3½" R strips.

Step 14. Cut nine 1½" by fabric with strips pink tonal. Join strips on short ends to make one long strip; press seams open. Subcut strip into two 95½" S strips and two 74½" T strips.

Step 15. Cut nine 6½" by fabric width strips large floral. Join strips on short ends to make one long strip; press seams open. Subcut strip into two 97½" U strips and two 86½" V strips.

Step 16. Cut (10) 2¼" by fabric width strips purple tonal for binding.

Completing the Green Star Blocks

Step 1. To complete one Green Star block, sew C to B and C to D on the short edges as shown in Figure 1; press seams toward B and D.

Figure 1   **Figure 2**

Step 2. Join the B-C unit with the C-D unit to complete a side unit as shown in Figure 2; press seam in one direction. Repeat for four side units.

Step 3. Sew a side unit to opposite sides of A to

complete the center row as shown in Figure 3; press seams toward A.

Figure 3   **Figure 4**

Step 4. Sew E to opposite sides of one side unit to complete the top row as shown in Figure 4; press seams toward E. Repeat for bottom row.

Step 5. Sew the top and bottom rows to the center row to complete the block center as shown in Figure 5; press seams away from the center row.

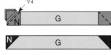

Figure 5   **Figure 6**

Step 6. Sew F to opposite sides of the block center; press seams toward F.

Step 7. Referring to Figure 6, sew an N square on each end of G on the marked line; trim seam to ¼" and press N to the right side to complete an N-G strip; repeat for two N-G strips.

Step 8. Sew an N-G strip to the remaining sides of the block center; press seams toward the N-G strips.

Step 9. Sew a K strip to an M strip to an L strip with right sides together along length to make a strip set; press seams in one direction. Repeat for six strip sets; subcut strip sets into (96) 2½" K-L-M units as shown in Figure 7.

Figure 7   **Figure 8**

Step 10. Join two K-L-M units with J as shown in Figure 8; press seams away from J. Repeat for four J-K-L-M units.

Step 11. Sew a J-K-L-M unit to opposite sides of the block center as shown in Figure 9; press seams toward the J-K-L-M units.

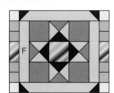

Figure 9

Step 12. Sew O to P along the diagonal to make a corner unit; press seam toward P. Repeat for four corner units.

Step 13. Sew a corner unit to each end of the remaining two J-K-L-M units as shown in Figure 10; press seams toward corner units. Sew these strips to the remaining sides of the block center as shown in Figure 11 to complete one Green Star block; press seams toward strips. Repeat for six Green Star blocks.

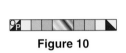

Figure 10

Figure 11

Completing the Lavender Star Blocks

Step 1. Repeat steps for Green Star blocks substituting H for D and I for E as shown in Figure 12 to complete six Lavender Star blocks.

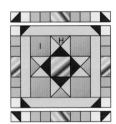

Figure 12

Completing the Top

Step 1. Join four R strips with one Lavender Star and two Green Star blocks to make a row referring to Figure 13; press seams toward R strips. Repeat for two rows.

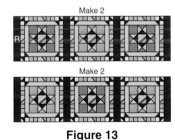

Figure 13

Step 2. Join four R strips with one Green Star and two Lavender Star blocks to make a row, again referring to Figure 13; press seams toward R strips. Repeat for two rows.

Step 3. Join three R strips with four Q squares to make a sashing row as shown in Figure 14; press seams toward R strips. Repeat for five sashing rows.

Figure 14

Step 4. Arrange the block rows with the sashing rows referring to the Placement Diagram for positioning of rows. **Note:** *In the sample shown, the two rows with the Green Star blocks in the middle are centered in the quilt top.*

Step 5. Sew an S strip to opposite long sides and T strips to the top and bottom of the pieced center; press seams toward S and T.

Step 6. Sew a U strip to opposite long sides and V strips to the top and bottom of the pieced center; press strips toward U and V to complete the pieced top.

Step 7. Complete the quilt referring to Completing Your Quilt on page 175. ★

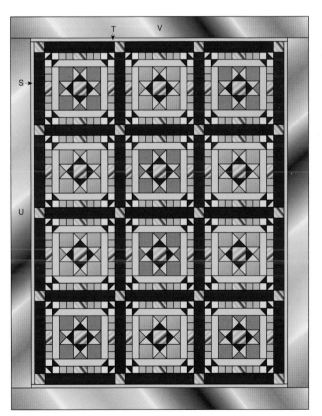

Stars in the Crossroads
Placement Diagram
86" x 109"

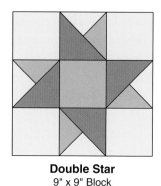

Double Star
9" x 9" Block

DESIGN BY
JILL REBER

Double Star Baby Quilt

Purple and yellow are a great combination in this pretty star-design baby quilt.

Project Specifications

Skill Level: Beginner
Quilt Size: 43" x 43"
Block Size: 9" x 9"
Number of Blocks: 9

Fabric & Batting

- ⅝ yard yellow print
- 1 yard dark purple print
- 1⅛ yards light purple print
- Backing 49" x 49"
- Batting 49" x 49"

Supplies & Tools

- Neutral color all-purpose thread
- Quilting thread
- Basic sewing tools and supplies

Cutting

Step 1. Cut one 3½" by fabric width strip light purple print; subcut strip into nine 3½" A squares.

Step 2. Cut two 3⅞" by fabric width strips dark purple print; subcut strips into (18) 3⅞" squares. Cut each square in half on one diagonal to make 36 B triangles.

Step 3. Cut one 4¼" by fabric width strip each light purple (C) and yellow (D) prints; subcut each strip into nine 4¼" squares. Cut each square on both diagonals as shown in Figure 1 to make 36 each C and D triangles.

Figure 1

Step 4. Cut three 3½" by fabric width strips yellow print; subcut strips into (36) 3½" E squares.

Step 5. Cut six 2" by fabric width strips light purple print; subcut strips into (24) 9½" F strips.

Step 6. Cut one 2" by fabric width strip yellow print; subcut strip into (16) 2" G squares.

Step 7. Cut four 5½" by fabric width strips dark purple print. Join strips on short ends to make one long strip; subcut strip into two 33½" H strips and two 43½" I strips.

Step 8. Cut five 2¼" by fabric width strips light purple print for binding.

Completing the Blocks

Step 1. Sew C to D on short sides to complete a C-D unit as shown in Figure 2; press seams toward C. Repeat for 36 C-D units.

| Figure 2 | Figure 3 |

Step 2. Sew B to a C-D unit to complete a side unit as shown in Figure 3; press seams toward B. Repeat for 36 side units.

Step 3. Sew a side unit to opposite sides of A to complete the center row as shown in Figure 4; press seams toward A.

Figure 4

Step 4. Sew E to opposite sides of a side unit to complete the top row as shown in Figure 5; press seams toward E. Repeat for bottom row.

Figure 5

Step 5. Sew the top and bottom rows to the center row referring to Figure 6 to complete one block; press seams toward the center row. Repeat for nine blocks.

Figure 6

Completing the Top

Step 1. Join three blocks with four F strips to make a block row as shown in Figure 7; repeat for three block rows. Press seams toward F.

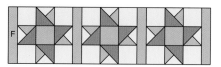

Figure 7

Step 2. Join three F strips with four G squares to make a sashing row as shown in Figure 8; press seams toward F. Repeat for four sashing rows.

Figure 8

Step 3. Join the block rows with the sashing rows, beginning and ending with a sashing row to complete the pieced center; press seams toward sashing rows.

Step 4. Sew an H strip to opposite sides and I strips to the top and bottom of the pieced center; press seams toward H and I.

Step 5. Complete the quilt referring to Completing Your Quilt on page 175. ★

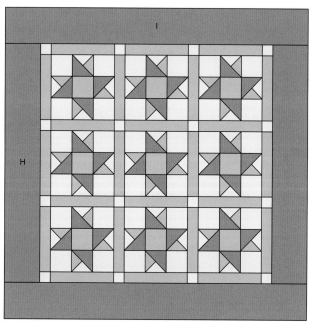

Double Star Baby Quilt
Placement Diagram
43" x 43"

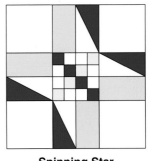

Spinning Star
12" x 12" Block

DESIGN BY
SANDRA L. HATCH

Spinning Stars

The complementary colors of blue and yellow in a beautiful iris print make a stunning quilt.

Project Specifications
Skill Level: Intermediate
Quilt Size: 76" x 76"
Block Size: 12" x 12"
Number of Blocks: 9

Fabric & Batting
- ¼ yard yellow tonal
- ½ yard blue/yellow stripe
- ¾ yard yellow/blue print
- 1¾ yards white tonal
- 2⅛ yards blue tonal
- 2¾ yards yellow/blue floral
- Backing 82" x 82"
- Batting 82" x 82"

Supplies & Tools
- Neutral color all-purpose thread
- Quilting thread
- Tri Recs tools (optional) or template material
- Basic sewing tools and supplies

Cutting
Step 1. Cut eight 1½" by fabric width A strips white tonal.

Step 2. Cut four 1½" by fabric width strips yellow (B) and blue (C) tonals.

Step 3. Cut five 4½" by fabric width strips yellow/blue print; subcut strips into (72) 2½" D rectangles.

Step 4. Cut three 4½" by fabric width strips each white (E and ER) and blue (F and FR) tonals. Prepare template for E/F using pattern given; use template as shown in Figure 1 to cut the required number of each piece as directed on the pattern.

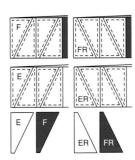

Figure 1

Note: *See page 91 for tips on Using Purchased Templates.*

Step 5. Cut four 4½" by fabric width strips white tonal; subcut strips into (36) 4½" G squares.

Step 6. Cut three 4½" by fabric width strips blue tonal; subcut strips into (12) 4½" H squares and (12) 2½" J rectangles.

Step 7. Cut one 12½" by fabric width strip white tonal; subcut strip into (12) 2½" K strips.

Step 8. Cut (11) 1½" by fabric width strips blue tonal. Join strips on short ends to make one long strip; press seams open. Subcut strip into two of each of the following strips: 52½" L, 54½" M, 58½" P and 60½" Q.

Step 9. Cut six 2½" by fabric width strips blue/yellow stripe. Join strips on short ends, matching stripes to continue design without interruption as shown in Figure 2; press seams open. Subcut strip into two 54½" N strips and two 58½" O strips.

Figure 2

Step 10. Cut four 8½" by fabric width strips yellow/blue floral. Join strips on short ends to make one long strip; subcut strip into two 76½" S strips.

Step 11. Cut two 8½" x 60½" R strips along the remaining length of the yellow/blue floral. *Note: The yellow/blue floral used in the sample is a directional print.*

Step 12. Cut four 8½" by fabric width strips yellow/blue floral. Join strips on short ends to make one long strip; subcut strip into two 76½" S strips.

Step 13. Cut eight 2¼" by fabric width strips blue tonal for binding.

Completing the Blocks

Step 1. Sew an A strip to a B strip with right sides together along length; press seams toward B. Repeat for four A-B strip sets. Subcut strip sets into (100) 1½" A-B segments as shown in Figure 3.

Figure 3

Step 2. Join two A-B segments to make an A-B unit as shown in Figure 4; repeat for 50 A-B units.

Figure 4

Step 3. Repeat Steps 1 and 2 with A and C strips to complete 100 A-C units, again referring to Figures 3 and 4. Set aside 32 each A-B and A-C units for sashing.

Step 4. To complete one Spinning Star block, sew an A-B unit to an A-C unit as shown in Figure 5; repeat for two units. Press seams toward A-C units.

Figure 5

Step 5. Join the pieced units to complete the center unit as shown in Figure 6; press seams in one direction.

Figure 6   **Figure 7**

Step 6. Sew E to F and ER to FR as shown in Figure 7; press seams toward F and FR. Repeat for two each E-F and ER-FR units.

Step 7. Sew D to each E-F and each ER-FR unit to complete the side and reversed side units as shown in Figure 8; press seams toward D.

Figure 8

Step 8. Sew a side unit to opposite sides of the center unit to complete the center row as shown in Figure 9; press seams away from the center unit.

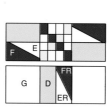   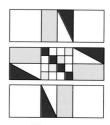
Figure 9   **Figure 10**

Step 9. Sew G to opposite sides of a reversed side unit to complete the top row, again referring to Figure 9; press seams toward G. Repeat for the bottom row.

Step 10. Sew the top and bottom rows to the center row as shown in Figure 10 to complete one Spinning Star block; press seams away from the center row. Repeat for nine blocks.

Completing the Sashing Units

Step 1. Sew an A-B unit to an A-C unit as shown in

Figure 11; press seams toward A-B units. Repeat for 32 A-B-A-C units.

Figure 11 **Figure 12**

Step 2. Join two A-B-A-C units to complete an A sashing unit as shown in Figure 12; press seams in one direction. Repeat for 16 units.

Step 3. Referring to Figure 7, sew E to F and ER to FR to complete 18 units each E-F and ER-FR; press seams toward F and FR.

Step 4. Sew D to 12 E-F units to make 12 D-E-F units referring to Figure 8; press seams toward D. Repeat for 12 D-ER-FR units, again referring to Figure 8.

Step 5. Join two D-E-F units with H to complete an H sashing unit as shown in Figure 13; press seams toward H. Repeat for six H sashing units. Repeat with two D-ER-FR units and H to complete one reversed H sashing unit, again referring to Figure 13; repeat for six reversed H sashing units.

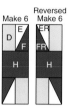

Figure 13 **Figure 14**

Step 6. Join one E-F unit with J and D as shown in Figure 14; press seams toward J. Add K to complete a K sashing unit, again referring to Figure 14; press seam toward K. Repeat for six units.

Step 7. Repeat Step 6 with ER-FR units to complete six reversed K units, again referring to Figure 14.

Completing the Top

Step 1. Join four A sashing units with three reversed H sashing units to make an H sashing row as shown in Figure 15; press seams toward the reversed H sashing units. Repeat for two H sashing rows.

Figure 15

Step 2. Join four A sashing units with three reversed K sashing units to make the top row as shown in Figure 16; press seams toward the K sashing units. Repeat for bottom row.

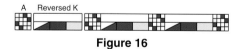

Figure 16

Step 3. Join two K sashing strips and two H sashing units with three blocks to complete a block row as shown in Figure 17; press seams away from blocks. Repeat for three block rows.

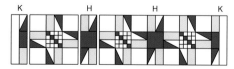

Figure 17

Step 4. Join the block rows with the top and bottom rows and sashing rows referring to Figure 18; press seams away from block rows.

Figure 18

Step 5. Sew an L strip to opposite sides and an M strip to the top and bottom of the pieced center; press seams toward L and M strips.

Step 6. Sew an N strip to opposite sides and an O strip to the top and bottom of the pieced center; press seams toward N and O strips.

Step 7. Sew a P strip to opposite sides and a Q strip to the top and bottom of the pieced center; press seams toward P and Q strips.

Step 8. Sew an R strip to opposite sides and an S strip to the top and bottom of the pieced center; press seams toward R and S strips to complete the top.

Step 7. Complete the quilt referring to Completing Your Quilt on page 175. ★

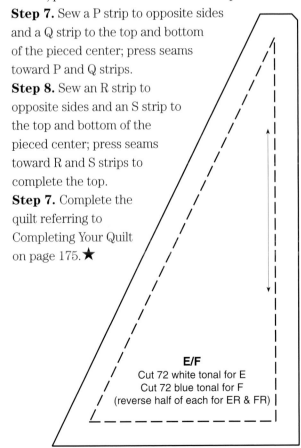

E/F
Cut 72 white tonal for E
Cut 72 blue tonal for F
(reverse half of each for ER & FR)

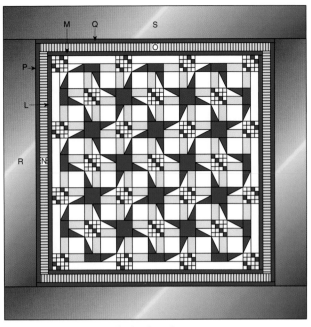

Spinning Stars
Placement Diagram
76" x 76"

Using Purchased Templates

Tri Recs templates may be used to cut the E and F pieces from fabric-width strips as shown in Photo 1. By simply placing the template on the strip at the line marked for the correct-size units, in this case 4½", it is easy to rotary-cut pieces. (Photo 1)

Reverse pieces are used in this pattern. Layer two strips with wrong sides together so that reverse pieces are cut at the same time. (Photo 2)

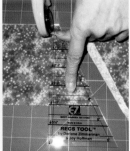

Photo 1　　　　**Photo 2**

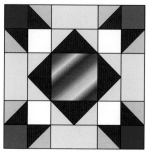

Stars in the Corners
18" x 18" Block
Make 10

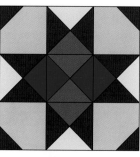

Star Four-Patch
18" x 18" Block
Make 10

DESIGN BY
JUDITH SANDSTROM

Starry Night

The black star points stand out like the night sky in this easy-to-stitch quilt.

Project Specifications
Skill Level: Beginner
Quilt Size: 83" x 101"
Block Size: 18" x 18"
Number of Blocks: 20

Fabric & Batting
- ½ yard white tonal
- 1 yard medium blue print
- 1⅜ yards red tonal
- 1¾ yards light blue tonal
- 2 yards pink tonal
- 2 yards multicolor print
- 2¼ yards black print
- Backing 89" x 107"
- Batting 89" x 107"

Supplies & Tools
- Neutral color all-purpose thread
- Quilting thread
- Basic sewing tools and supplies

Cutting
Step 1. Cut two 7¼" by fabric width strips each red

(A) and light blue (F) tonals and medium blue print
(B); subcut strips into (10) 7¼" squares each fabric.
Cut each square on both diagonals to make 40 each A,
B and F triangles.

Step 2. Cut seven 6½" by fabric width strips pink
tonal; subcut strips into (40) 6½" C squares.

Step 3. Cut four 3½" by fabric width strips black
print; subcut strips into (40) 3½" D squares. Mark a
diagonal line from corner to corner on the wrong side
of each square.

Step 4. Cut six 7¼" by fabric width strips black print;
subcut strips into (30) 7¼" squares. Cut each square
on both diagonals to make 120 E triangles.

Step 5. Cut two 6½" by fabric width strips multicolor
print; subcut strips into (10) 6½" G squares.

Step 6. Cut four 3½" by fabric width strips white
tonal; subcut strips into (40) 3½" H squares.

Step 7. Cut four 3⅞" by fabric width strips each
light blue (I) and pink (K) tonals and black print (L);
subcut strips into (40) 3⅞" squares each fabric. Cut
each square in half on one diagonal to make 80 each I,
K and L triangles.

Step 8. Cut four 6½" by fabric width strips light blue
tonal; subcut strips into (40) 3½" J rectangles.

Step 9. Cut two 3½" by fabric width strips each red tonal (M) and medium blue print (N); subcut strips into (20) 3½" squares each for M and N.

Step 10. Cut four 6" x 6" P squares medium blue print.

Step 11. Cut eight 6" by fabric width strips multicolor print. Join strips on short ends to make one long strip; press seams open. Subcut strips into two 90½" O strips and two 72½" Q strips.

Step 12. Cut (10) 2¼" by fabric width strips red tonal for binding.

Completing the Star Four-Patch Blocks

Step 1. To piece one block, sew A to E on one short side to make an A-E unit as shown in Figure 1; press seam toward E. Repeat for two A-E units.

Step 2. Repeat Step 1 with F and E to make an E-F unit, again referring to Figure 1. Repeat for four E-F units.

Figure 1

Figure 2

Step 3. Join one E-F unit with one A-E unit to complete an A side unit as shown in Figure 2; press seam in one direction. Repeat for two A side units.

Step 4. Repeat Steps 1–3 with B to make two B side units as shown in Figure 3.

Figure 3

Figure 4

Step 5. Place D on one corner of C and stitch on the marked line as shown in Figure 4. Trim seam to ¼"; press D to the right side to complete a corner unit, again referring to Figure 4. Repeat for four corner units.

Step 6. Sew A to the short side of B as shown in Figure 5 to make an A-B unit; press seam toward A. Repeat for two units.

Figure 5

Figure 6

Step 7. Join the two A-B units to complete the center unit as shown in Figure 6; press seam in one direction.

Step 8. Sew a corner unit to opposite sides of a B side unit to make a top row as shown in Figure 7; press seams toward the corner units. Repeat for bottom row.

Figure 7

Figure 8

Step 9. Sew an A side unit to opposite sides of the center unit to make the center row as shown in Figure 8; press seams toward the center unit.

Step 10. Sew the center row between the top and bottom rows to complete one Star Four-Patch block as shown in Figure 9; press seams away from the center row. Repeat for 10 blocks.

Figure 9

Completing the Stars in the Corners Blocks

Step 1. To complete one Stars in the Corners block, sew I to each short side of E to complete an E-I unit as shown in Figure 10; repeat for four E-I units.

Figure 10

Figure 11

Step 2. Sew J to an E-I unit to complete a side unit as shown in Figure 11; press seams toward J. Repeat for four side units.

Step 3. Sew K to L to make a K-L unit as shown in Figure 12; press seam toward L. Repeat for eight K-L units.

Figure 12

Figure 13

Figure 14

Step 4. Sew a K-L unit to M as shown in Figure 13; press seam toward M. Repeat with K-L and H, again referring to Figure 13; press seams toward H.

Step 5. Join the K-L-M unit with the K-L-H unit to complete an M corner unit as shown in Figure 14; press seam in one direction. Repeat for two M corner units.

Step 6. Repeat Steps 4 and 5 with N to complete two N corner units, again referring to Figure 14.

Step 7. Sew a side unit to opposite sides of G as shown in Figure 15 to complete the center row; press seams toward G.

Figure 15

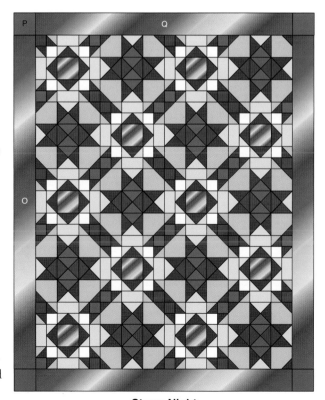

Figure 16

Step 8. Sew an M corner unit to one side of a side unit and an N corner unit to the other side as shown in Figure 16 to complete the top row; press seams toward corner units. Repeat for bottom row.

Step 9. Sew the center row between the top and bottom rows as shown in Figure 17 to complete one

Stars in the Corners block. Repeat for 10 blocks.

Completing the Top

Step 1. Join two Stars in the Corners blocks with two Star Four-Patch blocks to make a row as shown in Figure 18; press seams toward Stars in the Corners blocks. Repeat for five rows.

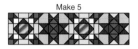

Figure 17

Make 5

Figure 18

Step 2. Join the rows referring to the Placement Diagram for positioning; press seams in one direction.

Step 3. Sew an O strip to opposite long sides of the pieced center; press seams toward O strips.

Step 4. Sew a P square to each end of each Q strip; press seams toward Q.

Step 5. Sew a Q-P strip to the top and bottom of the pieced center; press seams toward Q-P strips to complete the top.

Step 6. Complete the quilt referring to Completing Your Quilt on page 175. ★

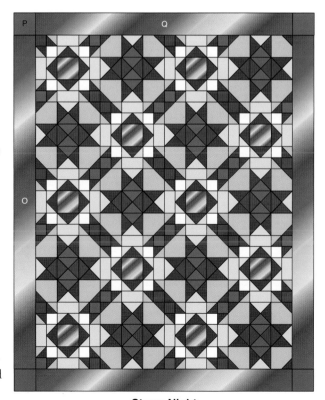

Starry Night
Placement Diagram
83" x 101"

Jewel of the Night
12" x 12" Block

DESIGN BY
SUE HARVEY

Jewel of the Night
Use strips to paper-piece the star and border units in this striking wall quilt

Project Specifications
Skill Level: Intermediate
Quilt Size: 19" x 19"
Block Size: 12" x 12"
Number of Blocks: 1

Fabric & Batting
- ¼ yard red mottled
- ⅓ yard yellow/black stripe
- ½ yard gold mottled
- 1¼ yards black mottled
- Backing 24" x 24"
- Batting 24" x 24"

Supplies & Tools
- Black all-purpose thread
- Quilting thread
- Basting spray
- Basic sewing tools and supplies

Cutting
Note: *Label all strips with letter and number; for example: S1, B1, etc., to indicate star (S) and border (B) strips.*

Step 1. Cut two 3¾" by fabric width S1 strips and two 3½" by fabric width S5 strips black mottled.

Step 2. Cut one fabric width strip for each size black mottled: 2" B1, 2¼" B3, 1¾" B5, 1½" B7 and 2¾" B9.

Step 3. Cut one 4⅜" by fabric width strip black mottled; subcut strip into two 4⅜" x 4⅜" A squares and four 2½" x 2½" E squares. Cut the A squares only in half on one diagonal to make four A triangles.

Step 4. Cut two 2" by fabric width strips black mottled; subcut strips into two 12½" B strips and two 15½" C strips.

Step 5. Cut two fabric width strips for each size yellow/black stripe: 2¼" S2 and 1¾" S4.

Step 6. Cut two 2¼" by fabric width S3 strips gold mottled.

Step 7. Cut one fabric width strip for each size gold mottled: 2¾" B2, 2½" B4, 2" B6 and 1¾" B8.

Step 8. Cut one 2" by fabric width S6 strip red mottled.

Step 9. Cut two 1" by fabric width strips red mottled; subcut strips into four 15½" D strips.

Step 10. Cut three 2¼" by fabric width strips black mottled for binding.

Paper-Piecing the Star Units

Step 1. Prepare eight copies of the star unit pattern; cut out, leaving about ⅛" all around outside line.

Step 2. Place an S1 strip right sides together with an S2 strip with right edges aligned and the S1 strip on top as shown in Figure 1.

Figure 1

Step 3. Place the unmarked side of one star-unit pattern on the layered strips with the line between the S1 and S2 sections ¼" in from the aligned edges of the strips as shown in Figure 2; pin in place.

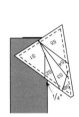

Figure 2   **Figure 3**

Step 4. Place another star-unit pattern on the layered strips just below the first pattern, overlapping patterns while leaving the S1/S2 line uncovered as shown in Figure 3; pin in place.

Step 5. Continue to pin patterns down the length of the strip.

Step 6. Using a stitch length of 15–18 stitches per inch or 1.5mm, stitch on the line between S1 and S2 sections beginning two stitches before the S3 intersecting line and ending at the outer line of the pattern as shown in Figure 4; do not cut thread.

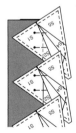   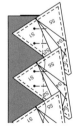

Figure 4   **Figure 5**

Step 7. Raise needle and presser foot and move to start stitching on the second pattern as shown in Figure 5; stitch along line as for the first pattern.

Continue in this manner with remaining patterns on strip.

Step 8. Repeat with remaining star-unit patterns with remaining S1 and S2 strips.

Step 9. Press S2 fabric over to cover S2 section of each pattern.

Step 10. Cut units apart along the bottom edge of each pattern.

Step 11. Fold the patterns back on the line between S1/S2 and S3 sections as shown in Figure 6; trim excess fabric ¼" from folded paper edge, again referring to Figure 6. Unfold patterns.

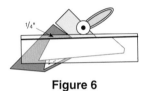

Figure 6

Step 12. Place the patterns with fabric side together with an S3 strip with the S3 line ¼" from the edge of the fabric strip as shown in Figure 7; pin pattern in place.

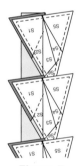

Figure 7

Step 13. Repeat along length of strip and on remaining S3 strip; stitch on the S3 lines as in Steps 6 and 7. Cut units apart.

Step 14. Press S3 over to cover S3 sections.

Step 15. Fold the patterns back on the S4 line; trim excess fabric ¼" from folded paper edge. Unfold patterns.

Step 16. Add S4, S5 and S6 pieces to each pattern in the same manner.

Step 17. When complete, trim the pattern and fabric even with the outer line of the pattern. Machine-baste around the outside edge within the ¼" seam allowance.

Completing the Block

Step 1. Place two units right sides together; align seam lines by poking a pin through both patterns at each end of the seam line as shown in Figure 8; pin units to hold.

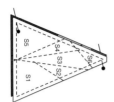

Figure 8

Step 2. Stitch on the seam line to join as shown in Figure 9. Remove paper in stitched seam allowance; press seam toward the S5 edge. Repeat to make four pairs.

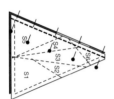

Figure 9

Step 3. Join two pairs; remove paper in seam allowance and press seam toward the S5 edge. Repeat.

Step 4. Join the two star halves; remove paper in seam allowance, split the seam at center and press both seam halves toward the S5 edges as shown in Figure 10.

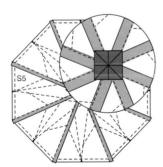

Figure 10

Step 5. Sew an A triangle to every other star unit edge to make block corners; press seams toward triangles. Trim triangles even with outer edges of star units to complete the block.

Completing the Top

Step 1. Sew a B strip to opposite sides of the block; press seams toward strips. Sew a C strip to the remaining sides; press seams toward strips.

Step 2. Remove paper patterns.

Step 3. Fold each D strip in half along length with wrong sides together; press.

Step 4. Place a strip along each outer edge of the bordered block with raw edges aligned and folded edge toward center of block; machine-baste in place within the ¼" seam allowance.

Step 5. Paper-piece four right border units and four left border units, beginning with B1 and B2 strips as for the star units. Trim the pattern and fabric even with the outer line of the pattern. Machine-baste around the outside edge within the ¼" seam allowance.

Step 6. Join a right and left border unit to make a strip as shown in Figure 11; press seam in one direction. Repeat to make four strips.

Figure 11

Step 7. Sew a strip to opposite sides of the center section referring to the Placement Diagram for positioning; remove paper in seam allowances and press seams toward strips. **Note:** *Be sure folded D strip stays flat against the inner border.*

Step 8. Sew an E square to each end of the remaining strips; press seams toward strips.

Step 9. Sew these strips to the remaining sides of the center section; remove paper in seam allowances and press seams toward strips.

Step 10. Remove paper patterns from borders.

Step 11. Complete the quilt using basting spray to hold layers together and referring to Completing Your Quilt on page 175. ★

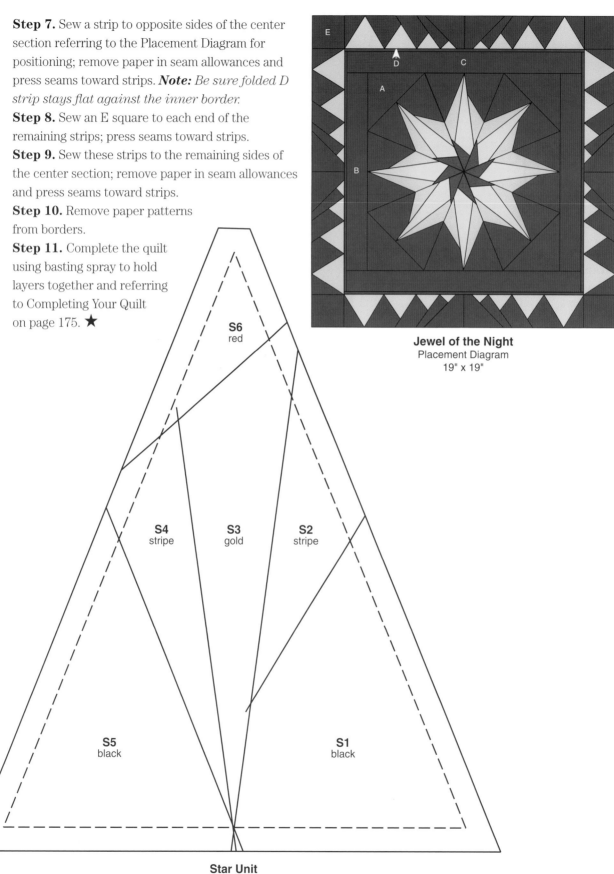

Jewel of the Night
Placement Diagram
19" x 19"

Star Unit
Make 8 copies

S6
red

S4
stripe

S3
gold

S2
stripe

S5
black

S1
black

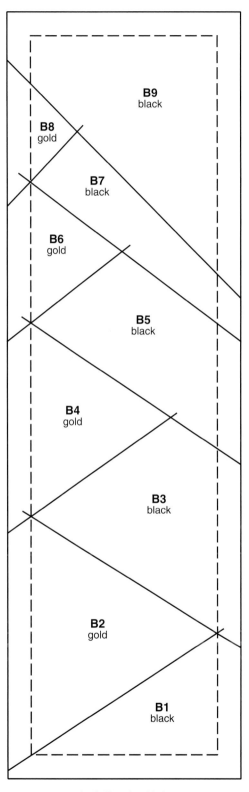

Left Border Unit
Make 4 copies

B9
black

B8
gold

B7
black

B6
gold

B5
black

B4
gold

B3
black

B2
gold

B1
black

Right Border Unit
Make 4 copies

B1
black

B2
gold

B3
black

B4
gold

B5
black

B6
gold

B7
black

B8
gold

B9
black

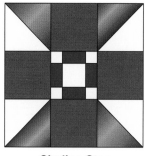

Circling Star
12" x 12" Block

DESIGN BY
SANDRA L. HATCH

Circling Stars of the Orient

Oriental prints hide the star design created by the sashing units of this pattern.

Project Specifications

Skill Level: Advanced
Quilt Size: 80" x 96"
Block Size: 12" x 12"
Number of Blocks: 20

Fabric & Batting

- ⅞ yard black/red metallic print
- 1⅝ yards cream solid
- 1¾ yards cream print
- 2¼ yards red print
- 3¼ yards black/cream print
- 3¼ yards Oriental print
- Backing 86" x 102"
- Batting 86" x 102"

Supplies & Tools

- Neutral color all-purpose thread
- Quilting thread
- Tri Recs templates or template material
- Basic sewing tools and supplies

Cutting

Step 1. Cut (14) 1½" by fabric width A strips cream solid.

Step 2. Cut (11) 1½" by fabric width B strips red print.

Step 3. Cut seven 1½" by fabric width C strips black/cream print.

Step 4. Cut two 2½" by fabric width strips each red print (D) and cream solid (E).

Step 5. Cut nine 4½" by fabric width strips black/cream print; subcut strips into (80) 4½" F squares.

Step 6. Cut five 4⅞" by fabric width strips each cream solid (G) and black/red metallic (H); subcut strips into (40) 4⅞" squares each fabric. Cut each square in half on one diagonal to make 80 each G and H triangles.

Step 7. Cut seven 4½" by fabric width strips each cream print (I and IR) and red print (J and JR). Prepare template for I/J using pattern given; cut as directed from strips using template referring to

Figure 1. **Note:** *See page 107 for tips on using purchased templates.*

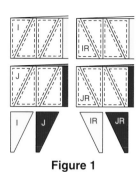

Figure 1

Step 8. Cut five 4½" by fabric width strips red print; subcut strips into (18) 2½" K rectangles and (31) 4½" M squares.

Step 9. Cut (10) 2½" by fabric width strips black/cream print; subcut strips into (160) 2½" L squares. Draw a diagonal line from corner to corner on the wrong side of each square.

Step 10. Cut five 4½" by fabric width N strips cream print. Prepare template for N using pattern given; cut 62 N pieces from strips referring to Figure 2. **Note:** *See page 107 for tips on using purchased templates.*

Figure 2

Step 11. Cut eight 1½" by fabric width strips black/cream print. Join strips on short ends to make one long strip; press seams open. Subcut strip into two 80½" O strips and two 66½" P strips.

Step 12. Cut four 6½" by fabric width strips Oriental print. Join strips on short ends to make one long strip; press seams open. Subcut strip into two 80½" R strips.

Step 13. Cut two 6½" x 84½" Q strips along remaining length of Oriental print.

Step 14. Cut nine 2¼" by fabric width strips black/cream print for binding.

Completing the Blocks

Step 1. Sew a D strip between two A strips with right sides together along length to make a strip set; press seams toward D. Repeat for two strip sets; subcut strip

sets into (40) 1½" A-D units as shown in Figure 3.

Figure 3   **Figure 4**

Step 2. Sew an E strip between two B strips with right sides together along length to make a strip set; press seams toward B. Repeat for two strip sets. Subcut strip sets into (20) 2½" B-E units as shown in Figure 4.

Step 3. Sew an A-D unit to each side of a B-E unit to complete a center unit as shown in Figure 5; repeat for 20 center units. Press seams toward A-D units.

Figure 5   **Figure 6**

Step 4. Sew G to H along the diagonal to make a corner unit as shown in Figure 6; repeat for 80 corner units. Press seams toward H.

Step 5. To complete one block, sew F to opposite sides of a center unit as shown in Figure 7 to complete the center row; press seams toward F.

Figure 7   **Figure 8**

Step 6. Sew a corner unit to opposite sides of F to complete the top row as shown in Figure 8; press seams toward F. Repeat for bottom row.

Step 7. Sew the top and bottom rows to the center row referring to Figure 9 to complete one Circling Star block; press seams toward the center row. Repeat for 20 blocks.

Figure 9   **Figure 10**

Completing the Sashing Units

Step 1. Sew J and JR to N to complete an N-J unit as shown in Figure 10; press seams toward J and JR. Repeat for 62 N-J units.

Step 2. Referring to Figure 11, sew L to opposite

corners of M on the marked lines; trim seams to ¼" and press M to the right side. Repeat on the remaining corners to complete an L-M unit. Repeat for 31 L-M units.

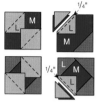 

Figure 11   **Figure 12**

Step 3. Sew an N-J unit to opposite sides of an L-M unit to complete an M sashing unit as shown in Figure 12; press seams toward L-M. Repeat for 31 M sashing units.

Step 4. Sew an A strip to a B strip with right sides together along length; press seams toward B. Repeat for three A-B strip sets. Subcut strip sets into (80) 1½" A-B segments as shown in Figure 13.

Figure 13   **Figure 14**

Step 5. Repeat Step 4 with A and C strips to complete three A-C strip sets; press seams toward C. Subcut strip sets into (80) 1½" A-C segments, again referring to Figure 13.

Step 6. Join two A-B segments to make an A-B unit as shown in Figure 14; press seam to one side. Repeat to make 40 A-B units. Repeat to make 40 A-C units, again referring to Figure 14.

Step 7. Set aside two each A-B and A-C units for top and bottom sashing rows. Join one each A-B and A-C units to complete an A-B-C unit as shown in Figure 15; press seam in one direction. Repeat for 38 A-B-C units.

Figure 15   **Figure 16**

Step 8. Join two A-B-C units to complete an A unit as shown in Figure 16; press seams in one direction. Repeat for 12 A units. Set aside remaining A-B-C units for sashing rows.

Step 9. Sew L to K as in Step 2 and referring to Figure 17 to complete an L-K unit; repeat for 18 units.

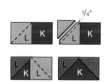

Figure 17   **Figure 18**

Step 10. Sew I to J to complete an I-J unit as shown in Figure 18; press seam toward J. Repeat for 18 I-J units. Repeat with IR and JR to complete 18 IR-JR units, again referring to Figure 18.

Step 11. Sew an I-J unit to one end and an IR-JR unit to the opposite ends of an L-K unit to complete an L sashing unit as shown in Figure 19; press seams away from L-K. Repeat for 18 K sashing units.

Figure 19

Completing the Top

Step 1. Join four Circling Stars blocks with three M and two K sashing units to make a block row as shown in Figure 20; press seams toward blocks. Repeat for five block rows.

Figure 20

Step 2. Join two A-B-C units with four M sashing units and three A sashing units to make a sashing row as shown in Figure 21; press seams toward A and A-B-C sashing units. Repeat for four sashing rows.

Figure 21

Step 3. Join one each A-B and A-C units, three A-B-C units and four K sashing units to complete the top sashing row as shown in Figure 22; press seams toward A-B, A-B-C and A-C units. Repeat for bottom sashing row.

Figure 22

Step 4. Join the block rows and sashing rows referring to Figure 23 to complete the pieced center; press seams toward block rows.

Step 5. Sew an O strip to opposite long sides and P strips to the top and bottom of the pieced center; press seams toward O and P strips.

Step 6. Sew an A strip to a C strip to a B strip with right sides together along length to make a strip set; press seams toward C. Repeat for four strip sets. Subcut strip sets into (100) 1½" border segments as shown in Figure 24.

Step 7. Remove a red square from two border segments.

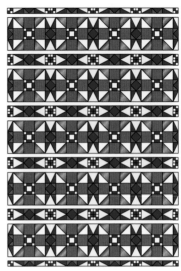

Figure 23

Figure 24

Step 8. Join 27 border segments on short ends and add a red square to the cream end to complete a side border strip as shown in Figure 25; press seams away from cream squares. Repeat for two side strips.

Step 9. Join 22 border segments on short ends and add the cream/black segment to the red end to complete an end border strip, again referring to Figure 25; press seams away from cream squares. Repeat for two end strips.

Step 10. Sew the side strips to opposite long sides and the end strips to the top and bottom of the pieced center referring to the Placement Diagram for positioning of strips; press seams toward O and P strips.

Step 11. Sew Q strips to opposite long sides and R strips to the top and bottom of the pieced center; press seams toward Q and R strips to complete the pieced top.

Step 12. Complete the quilt referring to Completing Your Quilt on page 175. ★

Figure 25

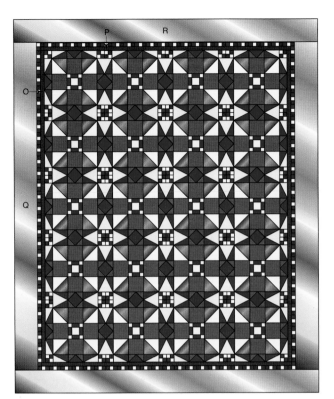

Circling Stars
Placement Diagram
80" x 96"

Using Purchased Templates

Tri Recs templates may be used to cut the I/J and N pieces from fabric-width strips as shown in Photo 1. By simply placing the N template on the strip at the line marked for the correct-size unit, in this case 4½", it is easy to rotary-cut pieces. (Photo 1)

Reverse I/J pieces are used in this pattern. Layer two strips with wrong sides together so that reverse pieces are cut at the same time. (Photo 2)

Photo 1   **Photo 2**

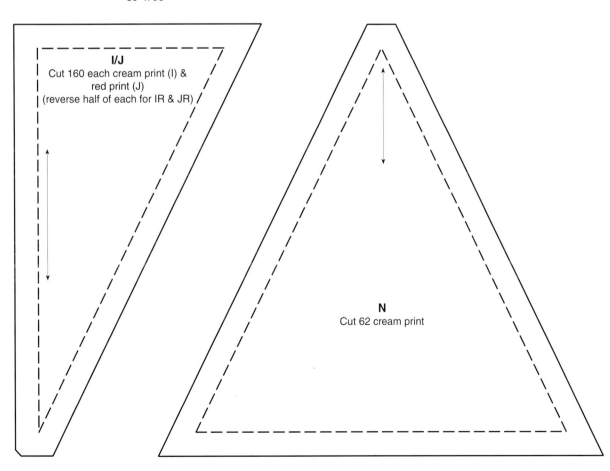

I/J
Cut 160 each cream print (I) &
red print (J)
(reverse half of each for IR & JR)

N
Cut 62 cream print

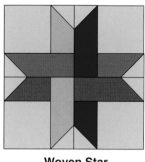

Woven Star
12" x 12" Block

DESIGN BY
JULIE WEAVER

Woven Stars

Fabric selection and placement create the illusion of woven pieces in this lovely bed-size quilt.

Project Specifications
Skill Level: Beginner
Quilt Size: 88" x 109¼"
Block Size: 12" x 12"
Number of Blocks: 18

Fabric & Batting
- ½ yard each red prints for A/E and D/H and blue prints for B/F and C/G
- 1⅛ yards red small floral
- 3½ yards tan print
- 5¼ yards red large floral
- Backing 94" x 115"
- Batting 94" x 115"

Supplies & Tools
- Neutral color all-purpose thread
- Quilting thread
- Basic sewing tools and supplies

Cutting
Step 1. Cut five 2½" by fabric width strips each fabrics A/E, B/F, C/G and D/H; subcut three strips each fabric into (18) 6½" A, B, C and D rectangles. Subcut the remaining two strips each fabric into (18) 4½" E, F, G and H rectangles.

Step 2. Cut nine 2½" by fabric width strips tan print; subcut strips into (144) 2½" I squares. Draw a diagonal line from corner to corner on the wrong side of each square.

Step 3. Cut eight 4½" by fabric width strips tan print; subcut strips into (72) 4½" J squares.

Step 4. Cut (39) 1½" by fabric width K strips tan print.

Step 5. Cut (24) 1½" by fabric width L strips red small floral.

Step 6. Cut three 22⅜" x 22⅜" squares red large floral; cut each square on both diagonals to make 12 O triangles. Discard two triangles.

Step 7. Cut two 13⅝" x 13⅝" squares red large floral; cut each square in half on one diagonal to make four P triangles.

Step 8. Cut nine 10½" by fabric width strips red large floral. Join strips on short ends to make one long

strip; press seams open. Subcut strip into two 89¾" Q strips and two 88½" R strips.

Step 9. Cut (10) 2¼" by fabric width strips red large floral for binding.

Completing the Blocks

Step 1. Arrange pieces in stacks for all blocks as shown in Figure 1.

Figure 1   **Figure 2**

Step 2. To complete one block, referring to Figure 2, place an I square right sides together on A and stitch on the marked line; trim seam to ¼" and press I to the right side to complete one A unit.

Step 3. Repeat Step 2 with I and F to complete an F unit referring to Figure 3.

Figure 3   **Figure 4**

Step 4. Sew J to the F unit as shown in Figure 4; press seam toward J.

Step 5. Add the A unit to the J-F unit to complete an A-F unit, again referring to Figure 4; press seam toward the J-F unit.

Step 6. Repeat Steps 2–5 with B and G, C and H, and D and E rectangles and I and J squares to complete remaining units referring to Figure 5.

Figure 5

Step 7. Arrange the units in rows referring to Figure 6. Join the A-F and B-G units; press seam toward the A-F unit. Repeat with the C-H and D-E units; press seam toward the C-H unit.

Step 8. Join the stitched units to complete one Woven Star block again referring to Figure 6 for positioning of units; press seams in one direction. Repeat for 18 blocks.

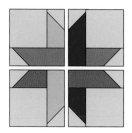

Figure 6

Completing the Sashing Units

Step 1. Sew an L strip between two K strips with right sides together along length to complete a K-L-K strip set referring to Figure 7; press seams toward L. Repeat for 18 strip sets.

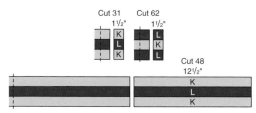

Figure 7

Step 2. Repeat Step 1 to make three L-K-L strip sets, again referring to Figure 7; press seams toward L.
Step 3. Subcut two K-L-K strip sets into (31) 1½" K segments, again referring to Figure 7. Repeat with the L-K-L strip sets to cut (62) 1½" L segments, again referring to Figure 7.
Step 4. Sew a K segment between two L segments to complete a sashing unit as shown in Figure 8; press seams in one direction. Repeat for 31 sashing units.

Figure 8

Step 5. Subcut the remaining K-L-K strip sets into (48) 12½" sashing strips, again referring to Figure 8.

Completing the Top

Step 1. Arrange the pieced blocks with the sashing units, the sashing strips and O and P triangles in diagonal rows referring to Figure 9; join to make

block rows and sashing rows; press seams toward the sashing strips and O and P triangles.

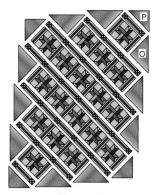

Figure 9

Step 2. Join the block rows with the sashing rows to complete the pieced center; press seams toward sashing rows.
Step 3. Sew a Q strip to opposite long sides and R strips to the top and bottom of the pieced center; press seams toward Q and R strips.
Step 4. Complete the quilt referring to Completing Your Quilt on page 175. ★

Woven Stars
Placement Diagram
88" x 109¼"

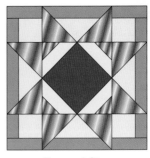

Framed Star
12" x 12" Block

DESIGN BY
JULIE WEAVER

Framed Stars

The star design in this quilt looks like it is setting on top of the frame that surrounds it.

Project Specifications

Skill Level: Intermediate
Quilt Size: 80" x 94"
Block Size: 12" x 12"
Number of Blocks: 20

Fabric & Batting

- ½ yard red check tonal
- 1 yard red print
- 1 yard yellow check tonal
- 2¼ yards blue tonal
- 2½ yards cream tonal
- 4⅔ yards large blue floral
- Backing 86" x 100"
- Batting 86" x 100"

Supplies & Tools

- All-purpose thread to match fabrics
- Quilting thread
- Basic sewing tools and supplies

Cutting

Step 1. Cut four 6½" by fabric width strips red print; subcut strips into (20) 6½" A squares.

Step 2. Cut seven 3½" by fabric width strips yellow check tonal; subcut strips into (80) 3½" B squares. Draw a line from corner to corner on the wrong side of each square.

Step 3. Cut four 2" by fabric width strips large blue floral; subcut strips into (80) 2" C squares. Draw a line from corner to corner on the wrong side of each square.

Step 4. Cut (14) 3½" by fabric width strips large blue floral; subcut strips into (160) 3½" D squares. Draw a line from corner to corner on the wrong side of each square.

Step 5. Cut (19) 1½" by fabric width F/H strips blue tonal.

Step 6. Cut three 3½" by fabric width strips blue tonal; subcut strips into (80) 1½" I rectangles.

Step 7. Cut (17) 1½" by fabric width K strips blue tonal.

Step 8. Cut two 2½" by fabric width strips blue tonal; subcut strips into (30) 2½" L squares.

Step 9. Cut (19) 2½" by fabric width E/G strips cream tonal.

Step 10. Cut (34) 1" by fabric width J strips cream tonal.

Step 11. Cut seven 1½" by fabric width strips red check tonal. Join strips on short ends to make one long strip; press seams open. Subcut strips into two 72½" M strips and two 60½" N strips.

Step 12. Cut eight 10½" by fabric width strips large blue floral. Join strips on short ends to make one long strip; press seams open. Subcut strips into two 74½" O strips and two 80½" P strips.

Step 13. Cut nine 2¼" by fabric width strips large blue floral for binding.

Completing the Blocks

Step 1. Referring to Figure 1, sew B to opposite corners of A on the marked line; trim seam to ¼" and press B to the right side. Repeat on the remaining corners of A to complete an A-B unit.

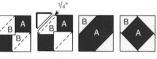

Figure 1

Step 2. Referring to Figure 2, repeat Step 1 with C squares to complete a center unit; repeat for 20 center units.

Figure 2

Step 3. Sew an E/G strip to an F/H strip with right

sides together along length; press seams toward F. Repeat for 19 strip sets.

Step 4. Subcut strip sets into (80) 6½" E-F units and (80) 2½" G-H units as shown in Figure 3.

Figure 3   **Figure 4**

Step 5. Referring to Figure 4 and Step 1, sew D to each end of an E-F unit to complete a side unit; repeat for 80 side units.

Step 6. Referring to Figure 5, sew I to G-H to complete a corner unit; press seam toward I. Repeat for 40 corner units and 40 reversed corner units.

Corner Unit
Make 40   Reversed
Corner Unit
Make 40

Figure 5

Step 7. To complete one block, sew a side unit to opposite sides of a center unit to make the center row as shown in Figure 6; press seams toward side units.

Figure 6

Step 8. Sew a corner unit and a reversed corner unit to opposite ends of a side unit to complete a side row as shown in Figure 7; press seams toward corner units. Repeat for two side rows.

Figure 7

Step 9. Sew a side row to opposite sides of the center row to complete one block; press seams toward side rows. Repeat for 20 blocks.

Completing Sashing Strips

Step 1. Sew a K strip between two J strips with right sides together along length; press seams toward K. Repeat for 17 strip sets.

Step 2. Subcut strip sets into (49) 12½" J-K sashing strips as shown in Figure 8.

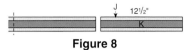

Figure 8

Completing the Top

Step 1. Join four blocks with five J-K sashing strips to complete a block row; press seams toward sashing strips. Repeat for five block rows.

Step 2. Join four J-K sashing strips with five L squares to complete a sashing row; press seams away from L. Repeat for six sashing rows.

Step 3. Join the block rows with the sashing rows to complete the pieced center; press seams toward sashing rows.

Step 4. Sew an M strip to opposite long sides and an N strip to the top and bottom of the pieced center; press seams toward M and N strips.

Step 5. Sew an O strip to opposite long sides and a P strip to the top and bottom of the pieced center; press seams toward O and P strips to complete the top.

Step 6. Complete the quilt referring to Completing Your Quilt on page 175. ★

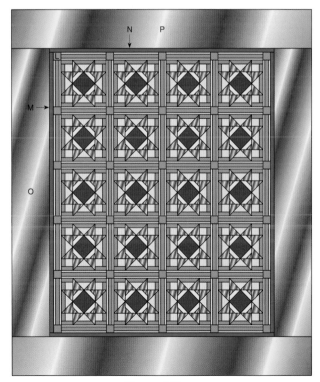

Framed Stars
Placement Diagram
80" x 94"

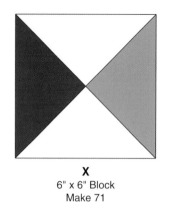

X
6" x 6" Block
Make 71

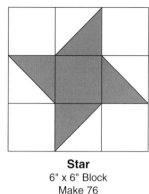

Star
6" x 6" Block
Make 76

DESIGN BY
CHRISTINE SCHULTZ

Back to the Fifties

Two simple blocks combine to make this
simple-to-stitch scrappy quilt.

Project Specifications
Skill Level: Beginner
Quilt Size: 78" x 90"
Block Size: 6" x 6"
Number of Blocks: 147

Fabric & Batting
Scraps used are from the 1950s era.
- 2⅓ yards purple print
- 3 yards total assorted scraps
- 4 yards white solid
- Backing 84" x 96"
- Batting 84" x 96"

Supplies & Tools
- Neutral color all-purpose thread
- Quilting thread
- Basic sewing tools and supplies

Cutting
Step 1. Cut (19) 2½" by fabric width strips white solid; subcut strips into (304) 2½" A squares.
Step 2. Cut (11) 2⅞" by fabric width strips white solid; subcut strips into (152) 2⅞" B squares. Draw a diagonal line from corner to corner on the wrong side of each square.
Step 3. For each star block, cut one 2½" x 2½" C square and two 2⅞" x 2⅞" D squares from the same scrap; repeat for 76 blocks.
Step 4. Cut eight 7¼" by fabric width strips white solid; subcut strips into (36) 7¼" squares. Cut each square on both diagonals to make 144 E triangles. Discard two triangles.
Step 5. Cut (36) 7¼" x 7¼" squares scraps; cut each square on both diagonals to make 144 F triangles. Discard two triangles.
Step 6. Cut two 6½" x 66½" G strips, two 6½" x 78½" H strips and five 2¼"-wide binding strips along the length of the purple print.

Completing the Star Block
Step 1. To complete one Star block, place a B square right sides together with a D square; stitch ¼" on each side of the marked line referring to Figure 1. Cut apart on the marked line and press open to make two B-D units, again referring to Figure 1. Repeat for four B-D units.

Figure 1

Step 2. Sew A to each side of two B-D units to make an A row as shown in Figure 2; press seams toward A. Repeat for two A rows.

Figure 2   **Figure 3**

Step 3. Sew a B-D unit to opposite sides of C to make the center row as shown in Figure 3; press seams toward C.

Step 4. Sew an A row to each side of the center row to complete one Star block as shown in Figure 4; press seams toward A rows. Repeat for 76 Star blocks.

Figure 4

Completing the X Blocks

Step 1. To complete one X block, sew F to E on the short sides as shown in Figure 5; press seam toward F. Repeat for two E-F units.

Figure 5

Step 2. Join the two E-F units as shown in Figure 6 to complete one X block; press seam in one direction. Repeat for 71 X blocks.

Figure 6

Completing the Top

Step 1. Join six Star blocks with five X blocks to make a star row referring to the Placement Diagram; press seams toward X blocks. Repeat for seven star rows.

Step 2. Join six X blocks with five Star blocks to make an X row referring to the Placement Diagram; press seams toward X blocks. Repeat for six X rows.

Step 3. Join the X and star rows, beginning and ending with a star row, to complete the pieced center; press seams in one direction.

Step 4. Sew an H strip to opposite sides of the pieced center; press seams toward H.

Step 5. Sew a Star block to each end of each G strip; press seams toward G. Sew a G-star strip to the top and bottom of the pieced center to complete the top; press seams toward G-star strips.

Step 6. Complete the quilt using the quilting designs given referring to Completing Your Quilt on page 175. ★

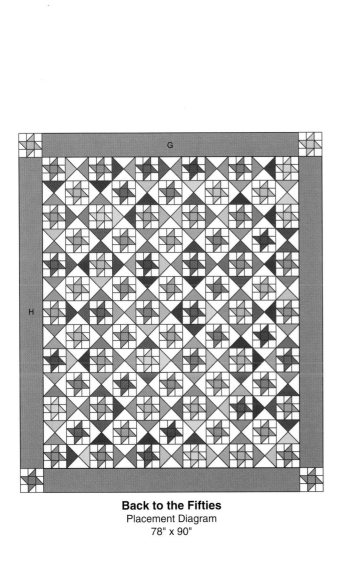

Back to the Fifties
Placement Diagram
78" x 90"

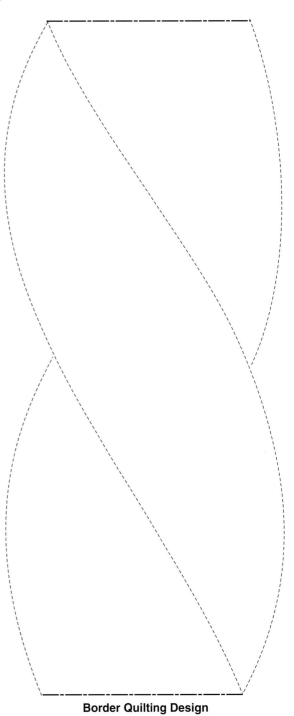

Border Quilting Design

Cable Quilting Design
Center around Star blocks.

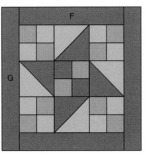

Spinning Star
8" x 8" Block
Make 6

Flying Geese
8" x 8" Block
Make 2

DESIGN BY
JILL REBER

Stars in Flight

The placement of the blocks in this quilt make it reminiscent of an old game board.

Project Specifications
Skill Level: Beginner
Quilt Size: 32" x 32"
Block Size: 8" x 8"
Number of Blocks: 8

Fabric & Batting
- 6 different fat eighths
- ¼ yard gold tonal
- ⅓ yard purple tonal
- ½ yard tan tonal
- ⅝ yard tan print
- Backing 38" x 38"
- Batting 38" x 38"

Supplies & Tools
- Neutral color all-purpose thread
- Quilting thread
- Basic sewing tools and supplies

Cutting
Step 1. Cut two 1½" by fabric width A strips and (12) 1½" x 1½" A squares gold tonal.

Step 2. Cut two 1½" x 1½" B squares from each of the six fat eighths.

Step 3. Cut three 2⅞" by fabric width strips tan tonal; subcut strips into (36) 2⅞" squares. Cut each square in half on one diagonal to make 72 C triangles.

Step 4. Cut two 2⅞" x 2⅞" squares from each of the six fat eighths; cut each square in half on one diagonal to make four D triangles each fabric.

Step 5. Cut two 1½" by fabric width E strips tan tonal.

Step 6. Cut two 1½" x 6½" F strips and two 1½" x 8½" G strips from each of the six fat eighths.

Step 7. Cut one 5¼" x 5¼" square from each of the six fat eighths; cut each square on both diagonals as shown in Figure 1 to make four H triangles of each fabric.

Figure 1

Step 8. Cut two 4½" x 24½" I strips and two 4½" x 32½" J strips tan print.

Step 9. Cut four 2¼" by fabric width strips purple tonal for binding.

Completing the Spinning Star Blocks

Step 1. Sew an A strip to an E strip with right sides together along length; press seams toward A. Repeat for two strip sets.

Step 2. Subcut strip sets into (48) 1½" A-E units as shown in Figure 2.

Figure 2   **Figure 3**

Step 3. Join two A-E units to complete a corner unit as shown in Figure 3; repeat for 24 units. Press seams in one direction.

Step 4. To complete one Spinning Star block, select same-fabric B, D, F and G pieces.

Step 5. Sew an A square to a B square; press seam toward B. Repeat for two units. Join the two units to complete the center unit as shown in Figure 4; press seam in one direction.

Figure 4   **Figure 5**

Step 6. Sew C to D to complete a side unit as shown in Figure 5; repeat for four side units. Press seams toward D.

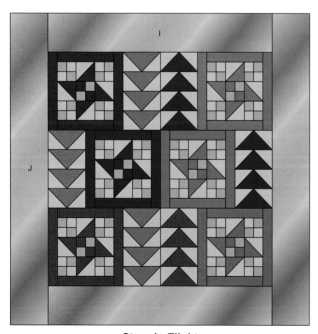

Stars in Flight
Placement Diagram
32" x 32"

Step 7. Sew the center unit between two side units to complete the center row as shown in Figure 6; press seam toward center unit.

Figure 6

Step 8. Sew a side unit between two corner units to make a top row, again referring to Figure 6; press seam toward corner units. Repeat for bottom row.

Step 9. Sew the center row between the top and bottom rows to complete one Spinning Star block; press seams toward center row. Repeat for six blocks.

Completing the Flying Geese Blocks

Step 1. Sew C to each short side of each H triangle as shown in Figure 7; press seams toward C.

Figure 7   **Figure 8**

Step 2. Select four same-fabric C-H units; join to complete a Flying Geese unit as shown in Figure 8; press seams in one direction. Repeat for six units.

Step 3. Join two Flying Geese units as shown in Figure 9 to complete one Flying Geese block; press seam in one direction. Repeat for two blocks. Remaining units are used as is to complete the top.

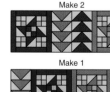

Figure 9   **Figure 10**

Completing the Top

Step 1. Sew a Flying Geese block between two Spinning Star blocks to complete a row referring to Figure 10; repeat for two rows. Press seams toward Spinning Stars blocks.

Step 2. Join two Spinning Star blocks with two Flying Geese units to make a row, again referring to Figure 10; press seams toward Flying Geese units and in one direction.

Step 3. Join the rows to complete the pieced center referring to the Placement Diagram for positioning;

press seams in one direction.

Step 4. Sew an I strip to opposite sides and J strips to the remaining sides of the pieced center; press seams toward strips.

Step 5. Complete the quilt referring to Completing Your Quilt on page 175. ★

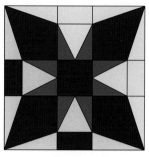

The Stars Inside
12" x 12" Block

DESIGN BY
SUE HARVEY

The Stars Inside

Trimmed seam allowances at template corners mean easy alignment of pieces and make stitching sharp star points a breeze.

Project Specifications
Skill Level: Intermediate
Quilt Size: 39" x 39"
Block Size: 12" x 12"
Number of Blocks: 4

Fabric & Batting
- Fat quarter red-violet batik
- Fat quarter gold batik
- ¾ yard light multicolor batik
- 1⅝ yards dark multicolor batik
- Backing 45" x 45"
- Batting 45" x 45"

Supplies & Tools
- Neutral color all-purpose thread
- Quilting thread
- Basic sewing tools and supplies

Cutting Instructions
Step 1. Prepare templates for A, B, C and D pieces using full-size patterns given.

Step 2. Cut three 5" by fabric width strips dark multicolor batik; place the A template on the strips as shown in Figure 1 and cut 16 dark A pieces. Place the B template on the remaining strip and cut four each dark B and BR pieces, again referring to Figure 1.

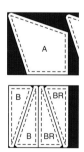

Figure 1

Step 3. Cut one 3½" by fabric width strip dark multicolor batik; subcut strip into eight 2" dark E rectangles and four 3½" F squares.

Step 4. Cut four 2" x 24½" H strips and two each 3½" x 33½" I and 3½" x 39½" J strips dark multicolor batik.

Step 5. Cut four 2¼" by fabric width strips dark multicolor batik for binding.

Step 6. Cut one 5" by fabric width strip light multicolor batik; cut four light A pieces and eight each light B and BR pieces from the strip as in Step 2 and Figure 1 for dark multicolor batik.

Step 7. Cut one 3½" by fabric width strip light multicolor batik; place the C template on the strip as shown in Figure 2 and cut eight light C pieces.

Figure 2

Step 8. Cut four 3½" by fabric width strips light multicolor batik; subcut strips into four 24½" G strips and eight 2" light E rectangles.

Step 9. Cut two 3½" x 22" strips red-violet batik; place the D template on the strips as shown in Figure 3 and cut 16 each D and DR pieces.

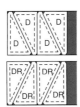

Figure 3

Step 10. Cut one 5" x 22" strip gold batik; cut eight each gold B and BR pieces from the strip as in Step 2 and Figure 1 for dark multicolor batik.

Step 11. Cut one 3½" x 22" strip gold batik; cut eight gold C pieces as in Step 7 and Figure 2 for light multicolor batik.

Piecing the Blocks

Step 1. Sew light B and BR pieces to the long sides of a dark A piece as shown in Figure 4; press seams toward B and BR. Repeat for four light corner units.

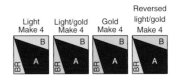

Figure 4

Step 2. Repeat with a light B and gold BR to make four light/gold corner units, a gold B and gold BR to make four gold corner units and a gold B and light BR to make four reversed light/gold corner units, again referring to Figure 4.

Step 3. Sew D and DR pieces to the long sides of a light C piece as shown in Figure 5; press seams toward D and DR. Add a light E to the C end to complete one light side unit, again referring to Figure 5; press seam toward E. Repeat for eight light side units.

Figure 5

Step 4. Repeat Step 3 with gold C and dark E pieces to make eight gold side units as shown in Figure 6.

Figure 6

Step 5. Sew F between one each light and gold side units to complete a center row as shown in Figure 7; press seams toward F. Repeat for four center rows.

Figure 7

Step 6. Sew a light side unit between one each light and light/gold corner units to make a top row as shown in Figure 8; press seams toward the corner units. Repeat for four top rows.

Figure 8

Step 7. Sew a gold side unit between one each gold and reversed light/gold corner units to make a bottom row as shown in Figure 9; press seams toward the corner units. Repeat for four bottom rows.

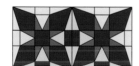

Figure 9

Step 8. Sew a center row between a top and bottom row to complete one block referring to the block drawing for positioning of rows; press seams in one direction. Repeat for four blocks.

Completing the Top
Step 1. Join two blocks to make a row as shown in Figure 10; press seam in one direction. Repeat for two rows.

Figure 10

Step 2. Join the rows to complete the pieced center; press seam open between rows.
Step 3. Sew G to H with right sides together along the length to make a G-H strip; press seam toward G. Repeat for four G-H strips.
Step 4. Sew a G-H strip to opposite sides of the pieced center referring to the Placement Diagram for positioning of strips; press seams toward strips.
Step 5. Sew dark B and BR pieces to the long sides of a light A as shown in Figure 11; press seams toward B. Repeat for four A-B units.

Figure 11

Step 6. Sew an A-B unit to each end of the remaining G-H strips as shown in Figure 12; press seams toward strips.

Figure 12

Step 7. Sew a strip to the remaining sides of the pieced center referring to the Placement Diagram for positioning of strips; press seams toward strips.
Step 8. Sew I to opposite sides and J to the remaining sides of the pieced center; press seams toward strips to complete the top.
Step 9. Complete the quilt referring to Completing Your Quilt on page 175. ★

The Stars Inside
Placement Diagram
39" x 39"

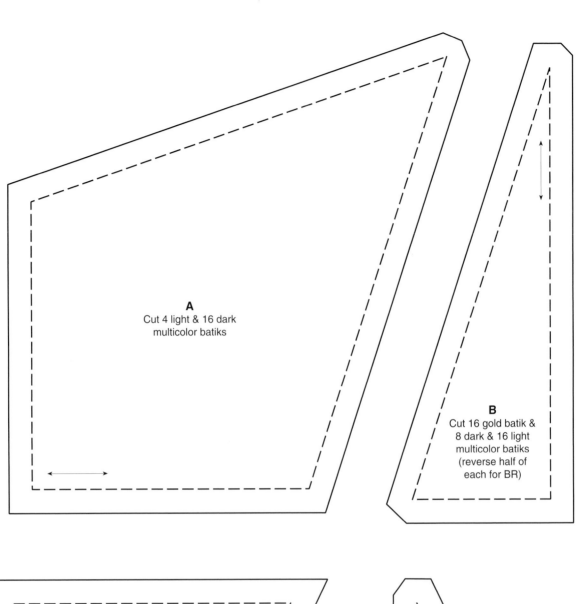

A
Cut 4 light & 16 dark
multicolor batiks

B
Cut 16 gold batik &
8 dark & 16 light
multicolor batiks
(reverse half of
each for BR)

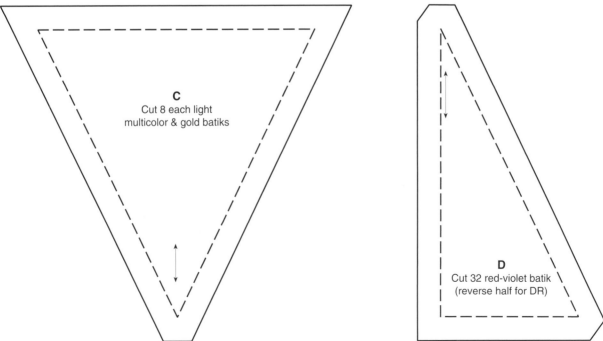

C
Cut 8 each light
multicolor & gold batiks

D
Cut 32 red-violet batik
(reverse half for DR)

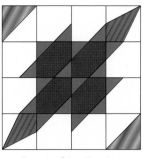
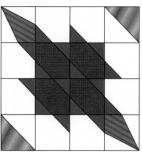

Purple Star Rocket
12" x 12" Block
Make 12

Blue Star Rocket
12" x 12" Block
Make 12

DESIGN BY
SUE HARVEY

Star Rockets in Flight

Use a trimming template to make accurate units for the sharp points in these blocks.

Project Specifications

Skill Level: Intermediate
Quilt Size: 66" x 90"
Block Size: 12" x 12"
Number of Blocks: 24

Fabric & Batting

- ⅔ yard blue/purple print
- ¾ yard each blue and purple mottleds
- 1½ yards black metallic
- 2⅛ yards blue/purple stripe
- 3½ yards white metallic
- Backing 72" x 96"
- Batting 72" x 96"

Supplies & Tools

- Neutral color all-purpose thread
- Quilting thread
- Basic sewing tools and supplies

Cutting

Step 1. Cut (16) 3½" by fabric width strips white metallic; subcut strips into (192) 3½" A squares.

Step 2. Cut three 3⅞" by fabric width strips white metallic; subcut strips into (24) 3⅞" E squares.

Step 3. Cut five 4½" by fabric width strips white metallic; subcut strips into (48) 3¾" rectangles. Cut each rectangle in half on one diagonal to make 48 each H and HR pieces as shown in Figure 1.

Make 48   Make 48

Figure 1

Step 4. Cut seven 3½" by fabric width strips white metallic; subcut strips into six 24½" J strips and four each 12½" K strips and 15½" L strips.

Step 5. Cut (10) 2" by fabric width strips blue mottled; subcut strips into (192) 2" B squares.

Step 6. Cut (10) 2" by fabric width strips purple mottled; subcut strips into (192) 2" C squares.

Step 7. Cut eight 3½" by fabric width strips black metallic; subcut strips into (96) 3½" D squares.

Step 8. Cut eight 2¼" by fabric width strips black metallic for binding.

Step 9. Cut three 3⅞" by fabric width strips blue/

purple print; subcut strips into (24) 3⅞" F squares.

Step 10. Cut two 3½" by fabric width strips blue/purple print; subcut strips into (20) 3½" I squares.

Step 11. Cut three 5¼" by fabric width strips blue/purple stripe; unfold strips and press flat. Layer strips with right sides up; cut into (24) 4" rectangles. Cut each rectangle in half on one diagonal to make 48 G pieces as shown in Figure 2.

Figure 2

Step 12. Cut eight 6½" by fabric width strips blue/purple stripe for M and N borders.

Piecing the Units

Step 1. Place H right sides together with the square corner edge of G, with points of G and H aligned as shown in Figure 3; stitch along edge. Press seam toward H.

Figure 3

Step 2. Place HR right sides together with the long angled edge of G, with points aligned as shown in Figure 4; stitch along edge. Press seam toward HR to complete one G-H unit, again referring to Figure 4. Repeat to make 48 G-H units.

Figure 4

Step 3. Prepare a template for the corner unit using the Trimming Template given on page 133.

Step 4. Place the template on a G-H unit, aligning the point of G and the seam lines between G and H and HR on the template with the stitched unit as shown in Figure 5.

Figure 5

Step 5. Using a rotary ruler, trim excess fabric around template to complete one corner unit as shown in Figure 6; repeat to trim all G-H units.

Figure 6

Step 6. Draw a diagonal line from corner to corner on the wrong side of each B, C, E and I square.

Step 7. Place B right sides together on one corner of A as shown in Figure 7; stitch on the marked line, trim seam allowance to ¼" and press B open to complete an A-B unit, again referring to Figure 7. Repeat to make 96 A-B units.

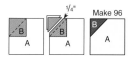

Figure 7

Step 8. Repeat Step 7 with C and A squares to complete 96 A-C units as shown in Figure 8.

Step 9. Repeat Step 7 with a B square on opposite corners of D to complete 48 B-D units, again referring to Figure 8.

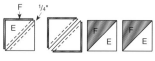

Figure 8

Step 10. Repeat Step 7 with a C square on opposite corners of D to complete 48 C-D units, again referring to Figure 8.

Step 11. Place E right sides together with F; stitch ¼" from each side of the marked line as shown in Figure 9; cut on the marked line and press seam toward F to complete two E-F units, again referring to Figure 9. Repeat to make 48 E-F units.

Figure 9

Piecing the Blocks

Step 1. To complete one Blue Star Rocket block, join two A-B units with one each corner unit and E-F

Press seams between rows as indicated by arrows in Figure 12. Repeat to make 12 blue blocks.

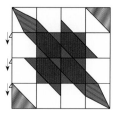

Figure 12

Step 4. Repeat Steps 1–3 using A-C and C-D units with the corner units and E-F units to complete one Purple Star Rocket block referring to arrows in Figure 13 to press seams between rows. Repeat to make 12 purple blocks.

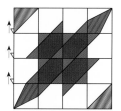

Figure 13

Completing the Top

Step 1. Join two each blue and purple blocks to make a block row as shown in Figure 14; press seams toward blue blocks. Repeat to make six block rows.

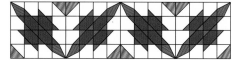

Figure 14

Step 2. Join the rows to complete the pieced center referring to the Placement Diagram for positioning of rows; press seams in one direction.

Step 3. Place I right sides together on each end of J as shown in Figure 15; stitch, trim and press I open to complete one I-J strip, again referring to Figure 15. Repeat to make six I-J strips.

Figure 15

Step 4. Place I right sides together on one end of each K and L strip, stitch, trim and press I open to

unit to make a top row as shown in Figure 10; press seams as indicated by arrows in Figure 10. Repeat for a bottom row.

Figure 10

Step 2. Join two B-D units with two A-B units to complete a center row as shown in Figure 11; press seams as indicated by arrows in Figure 11. Repeat for two center rows.

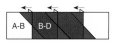

Figure 11

Step 3. Join the rows to complete one block as shown in Figure 12, turning rows to offset seams.

complete two each I-K, reversed I-K, I-L and reversed I-L units as shown in Figure 16.

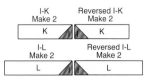

Figure 16

Step 5. Join two I-J strips with one each I-K and reversed I-K units to make a side border strip as shown in Figure 17; repeat for two strips. Press seams in one direction.

Step 6. Sew a strip to opposite long sides of the pieced center referring to the Placement Diagram for positioning of strips; press seams toward strips.

Step 7. Join one each I-J, I-L and reversed I-L units to make an end border strip, again referring to Figure 17; repeat for two strips. Press seams in one direction.

Step 8. Sew a strip to each end of the pieced center; press seams toward strips.

Step 9. Join the M/N border strips on short ends to make a long strip; press seams in one direction. Cut into two each 71" N strips and 95" M strips.

Step 10. Center and sew an M strip to opposite long sides, beginning and ending stitching ¼" from each corner; repeat with the N strips on each end.

Step 11. Miter border corners; trim excess at corners to ¼" and press open.

Step 12. Press border strips toward M and N to complete the top.

Step 13. Complete the quilt referring to Completing Your Quilt on page 175. ★

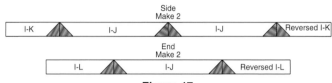

Figure 17

Trimming Template

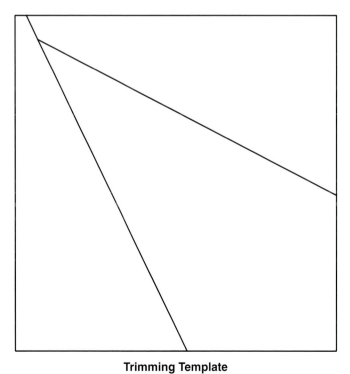

Star Rockets in Flight
Placement Diagram
66" x 90"

Starflower
10" x 10" Block

DESIGN BY
JULIE WEAVER

Starflowers Quilt

The points of a simple pieced star-design block form the leaves of the appliquéd flowers in this quilt made with 1930s reproduction prints.

Project Specifications
Skill Level: Intermediate
Quilt Size: 70" x 94"
Block Size: 10" x 10"
Number of Blocks: 24

Fabric & Batting
- 3 yards cream tonal
- 4¼ yards green dot
- 4¼ yards total assorted 1930s reproduction prints
- Backing 76" x 100"
- Batting 76" x 100"

Supplies & Tools
- Neutral color all-purpose thread
- Quilting thread
- 4 yards fusible web
- Basic sewing tools and supplies

Cutting
Step 1. Cut four 5½" by fabric width strips green dot; subcut strips into (24) 5½" A squares.

Step 2. Cut (14) 3" by fabric width strips green dot; subcut strips into (192) 3" C squares. Draw a diagonal line from corner to corner on the wrong side of each square.

Step 3. Cut seven 5½" by fabric width strips cream tonal; subcut strips into (96) 3" B rectangles.

Step 4. Cut seven 3" by fabric width strips cream tonal; subcut strips into (96) 3" D squares.

Step 5. Cut (11) 2½" by fabric width strips green dot; subcut three strips into (35) 2½" I squares. Join the remaining strips on short ends to make one long strip; subcut strip into two 74½" J strips and two 54½" K strips.

Step 6. Cut (15) 1" by fabric width G strips green dot.

Step 7. Cut (30) 1¼" by fabric width H strips cream tonal.

Step 8. Cut (176) 2" x 8½" L rectangles from assorted 1930s reproduction prints.

Step 9. Cut four 8½" x 8½" M squares green dot.

Step 10. Cut nine 2¼" by fabric width strips green dot for binding.

Step 11. Trace E and FF pieces given onto the paper side of the fusible web referring to patterns for number to cut; cut out circle shapes, leaving a margin around each one. Cut out FF shapes on traced lines.

Step 12. Bond circle shapes to the wrong side of green dot as directed on patterns for color; cut out shapes on traced lines. Remove paper backing.

Step 13. Prepare template for F; cut as directed on pattern.

Completing the Blocks

Step 1. To complete one block, referring to Figure 1, place a C square right sides together on one end of B; stitch on the drawn line. Trim seam allowance to ¼"; press C to the right side. Repeat on the other end of B to complete a B-C unit; repeat for four B-C units.

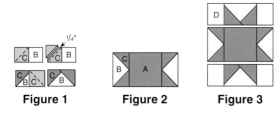

| Figure 1 | Figure 2 | Figure 3 |

Step 2. Sew a B-C unit to opposite sides of A as shown in Figure 2; press seams toward A.

Step 3. Sew a D square to each end of each of the remaining B-C units; press seams toward D. Repeat for two B-C-D units.

Step 4. Sew a B-C-D unit to opposite sides of the A-B-C unit as shown in Figure 3; press seams toward the A-B-C unit.

Step 5. Select eight assorted F petals. Join the petals on the straight edges to form a petal circle as shown in Figure 4.

| Figure 4 | Figure 5 |

Step 6. Place an FF fusible web piece on the wrong side of each petal in the petal circle; fuse in place. Remove paper backing.

Step 7. Position the petal circle on the pieced square as shown in Figure 5; when satisfied with placement, fuse in place.

Step 8. Center and fuse an E circle on the fused F pieces on top of the A square.

Step 9. Machine-stitch circle and curved petal edges in place using a blanket or buttonhole stitch and a neutral color thread to complete one Starflower block; repeat for 24 blocks.

Completing the Sashing Units

Step 1. Sew a G strip between two H strips with right sides together along length to make a G-H strip set; press seams toward G. Repeat for 15 strip sets.

Step 2. Subcut G-H strip sets into (58) 10½" sashing units as shown in Figure 6.

Figure 6

Completing the Top

Step 1. Join four Starflower blocks with five sashing units to complete a row; press seams toward sashing units. Repeat for six rows.

Step 2. Join four sashing units with five I squares to complete a sashing row; press seams away from I. Repeat for seven sashing rows.

Step 3. Join the block rows with the sashing rows, beginning and ending with a sashing row, to complete the pieced center; press seams toward sashing rows.

Step 4. Sew J strips to opposite sides and K to the top and bottom of the pieced center; press seams toward J and K.

Step 5. Join 52 L strips to make a side L strip; press seams in one direction. Repeat for two strips.

Step 6. Sew a side L strip to opposite sides of the pieced center; press seams toward L strips.

Step 7. Repeat Step 5 with 36 L strips to make top and bottom L strips. Sew an M square to each end of each strip; press seams away from M. Sew these strips to the top and bottom of the pieced center to complete the pieced top.

Step 8. Complete the quilt referring to Completing Your Quilt on page 175. ★

Starflowers Quilt
Placement Diagram
70" x 94"

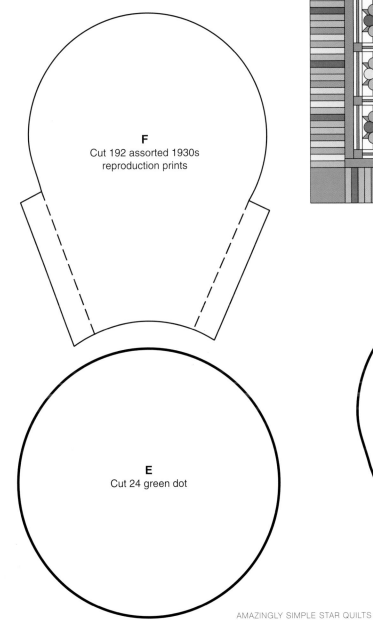

F
Cut 192 assorted 1930s
reproduction prints

E
Cut 24 green dot

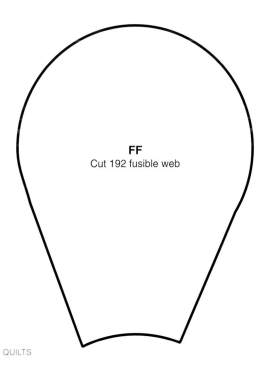

FF
Cut 192 fusible web

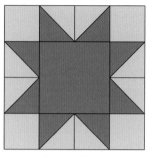

Large Star
16" x 16" Block
Make 5

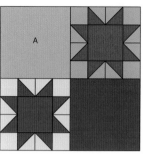

Four-Patch Star
16" x 16" Block
Make 4

DESIGN BY
KATE LAUCOMER

Homespun Stars

Homespun plaids and stripes in brushed cotton make a snuggly throw.

Project Note

The designer prefers to cut all the pieces for one star block or unit at one time and then store the pieces in a plastic zipper bag until the piecing step. This organizes the pieces to avoid trying to gather up the right pieces during the piecing process.

Project Specifications

Skill Level: Beginner
Quilt Size: 59" x 59"
Block Size: 16" x 16"
Number of Blocks: 9

Fabric & Batting

For each of the five Large Star blocks you will need:
- ¼ yard or 1 fat quarter light fabric for background
- ⅓ yard or 1 fat quarter dark fabric for star

For each of the eight small star units you will need:
- ⅛ yard light fabric for background
- ⅙ yard or 1 fat eighth (9" x 22") dark fabric for star

To complete the top, you will need:
- 8 (8½" x 8½") dark squares for A
- Red scraps to total ⅜ yard
- 1⅞ yards black plaid

- Backing 65" x 65"
- Batting 65" x 65"

Supplies & Tools

- Neutral color all-purpose thread
- Quilting thread
- Basic sewing tools and supplies

Cutting

Step 1. For each Large Star block, cut the following: four 4½" x 4½" C squares and four 4⅞" x 4⅞" D squares light background fabric and one 8½" x 8½" B square and four 4⅞" x 4⅞" E squares dark star fabric. Cut pieces for five blocks.

Step 2. For each small star unit, cut the following: four 2½" x 2½" G squares and four 2⅞" x 2⅞" H squares light background fabric and one 4½" x 4½" F square and four 2⅞" x 2⅞" I squares dark star fabric. Cut pieces for eight small star units.

Step 3. Cut 1½"-wide red scrap strips and join on short ends to make two 1½" x 48½" J strips and two 1½" x 50½" K strips.

Step 4. Cut two 5" x 50½" L strips and two 5" x 59½" M strips along the length of the black plaid.

Step 5. Cut four 2¼"-wide strips along the length of the black plaid for binding.

Completing the Large Star Blocks

Step 1. To complete one Large Star block, select matching B and E and C and D pieces. Draw a diagonal line from corner to corner on the wrong side of each D square.

Step 2. Place E right sides together with D; stitch ¼" on each side of the marked line as shown in Figure 1. Repeat for four D-E units.

Figure 1 **Figure 2**

Step 3. Cut the D-E units apart on the drawn line and press open as shown in Figure 2 to complete a total of eight D-E units.

Step 4. Join two D-E units as shown in Figure 3 to complete a side unit; repeat for four side units. Press seams in one direction.

Figure 3

Step 5. Sew a side unit to opposite sides of B to complete the center row as shown in Figure 4; press seams toward B.

Figure 4

Step 6. Sew C to each end of each remaining side unit; press seams toward C.

Step 7. Sew the C side units to the remaining sides of the center row as shown in Figure 5 to

complete one Large Star block; press seams toward the center row. Repeat for five blocks.

Figure 5

Completing the Four-Patch Star Blocks
Step 1. Repeat Steps 1–3 with the H and I squares to complete 64 H-I units as shown in Figure 6.

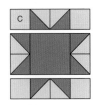

Figure 6   **Figure 7**

Step 2. To complete one star unit, join two matching H-I units to make a side unit as shown in Figure 7; press seams in one direction. Repeat for four side units.

Step 3. Sew a side unit to opposite sides of a matching F square to complete the center row as shown in Figure 8; press seams toward F.

Figure 8

Step 4. Sew matching G squares to each end of each remaining side unit; press seams toward G.

Step 5. Sew a G side unit to opposite sides of the center row as shown in Figure 9; press seams toward the center row. Repeat for two star units.

Figure 9

Step 6. Sew a star unit to A to make a row; press seam toward A. Repeat for two rows. Join the two rows to complete one Four-Patch Star block referring to the block drawing for positioning; press seam in one direction. Repeat for four blocks.

Completing the Top
Step 1. Join two Large Star blocks and one

Four-Patch Star block to complete one row as shown in Figure 10; press seams toward the Four-Patch Star block. Repeat for two rows.

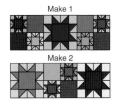

Figure 10

Step 2. Join two Four-Patch Star blocks with one Large Star block to complete a row, again referring to Figure 10; press seams toward Four-Patch Star blocks.

Step 3. Join the rows referring to the Placement Diagram to complete the pieced top; press seams in one direction.

Step 4. Sew J strips to opposite sides and K strips to the remaining sides of the pieced center; press seams toward J and K strips.

Step 5. Sew L strips to opposites sides and M strips to the top and bottom of the pieced center; press seams toward L and M strips.

Step 6. Complete the quilt referring to Completing Your Quilt on page175. ★

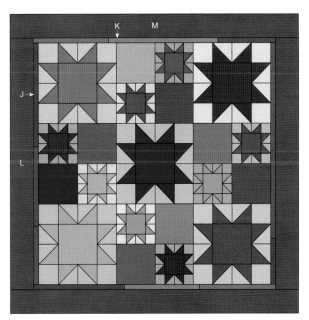

Homespun Stars
Placement Diagram
59" x 59"

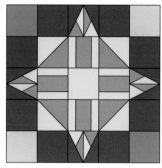

Four-Patch Galaxy
15" x 15" Block

DESIGN BY
CONNIE RAND

Four-Patch Galaxy

Squares in the corners of this star design make Four-Patches where the blocks meet.

Project Specification
Skill Level: Intermediate
Quilt Size: 78" x 93"
Block Size: 15" x 15"
Number of Blocks: 20

Materials
- ½ yard medium blue mottled
- ½ yard light blue mottled
- 1⅔ yards gold mottled
- 2¾ yards yellow mottled
- 4½ yards blue metallic
- Backing 84" x 99"
- Batting 84" x 99"

Supplies & Tools
- All-purpose thread to match fabrics
- Quilting thread
- Basic sewing tools and supplies

Cutting
Step 1. Cut (14) 3½" by fabric width strips blue metallic; subcut strips into (160) 3½" G squares.

Step 2. Cut two 6½" x 81½" M strips and two 6½" x 66½" N strips along remaining length of blue metallic.

Step 3. Cut four 3⅞" by fabric width strips yellow mottled; subcut strips into (40) 3⅞" squares. Cut each square in half on one diagonal to make 80 C triangles.

Step 4. Cut (14) 1½" by fabric width E strips yellow mottled.

Step 5. Cut nine 3½" by fabric width strips yellow mottled; subcut two of the strips into (20) 3½" J squares. Join remaining strips on short ends to make one long strip; press seams open. Subcut strip into two 75½" K strips and two 66½" L strips.

Step 6. Cut four 3⅞" by fabric width strips gold mottled; subcut strips into (40) 3⅞" squares. Cut each square in half on one diagonal to make 80 D triangles.

Step 7. Cut seven 2½" by fabric width F strips gold mottled.

Step 8. Cut four 3½" by fabric width strips each medium blue (H) and light blue (I) mottleds; subcut strips into (48) 3½" squares each H and I.

Step 9. Cut five 2¼"-wide strips along remaining length of blue metallic for binding.

Step 10. Refer to the General Instructions for paper-piecing for cutting instructions for A and B units.

Completing the Four-Patch Galaxy Blocks
Step 1. Make 80 copies each of Paper-Piecing Patterns A and B; cut out, leaving paper beyond the outside line of each pattern.

Step 2. Complete 80 A units and 80 B units referring to the General Instructions for paper piecing on page 173 and Figure 1.

A unit B unit
Make 80 Make 80

Figure 1

Step 3. Join C and D triangles to complete a C-D unit as shown in Figure 2; press seam toward D. Repeat for 80 C-D units.

Make 80

C
D

Figure 2

Step 4. Sew an F strip between two E strips with right sides together along length to make a strip set; press seams toward F. Repeat for seven strip sets. Subcut strip sets into (80) 3½" E-F units as shown in Figure 3.

3½"

E
F

Figure 3

Step 5. To piece one block, join two G squares with one each H and I squares and one each A and B units to make a row as shown in Figure 4; press seams toward G squares. Repeat for two rows.

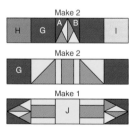

Make 2

H | G | A B | | I

Make 2

G

Make 1

J

Figure 4

Step 6. Join two G squares, two C-D units and one E-F unit to make a row, again referring to Figure 4; press seams away from C-D. Repeat for two rows.

Step 7. Join two each A and B units, two E-F units and one J square to make a center row, again referring to Figure 4; press seams toward E-F.

Step 8. Join rows to complete one Four-Patch Galaxy block as shown in Figure 5; press seams in one direction. Repeat to make 20 blocks.

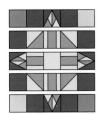

Figure 5

Completing the Top

Step 1. Join four blocks to make a row; press seams in one direction. Repeat for five rows.

Step 2. Join the rows to complete the pieced center; press seams in one direction.

Step 3. Sew the K strips to opposite long sides and L strips to the top and bottom of the pieced center; press seams toward K and L strips.

Step 4. Sew an M strip to opposite long sides of the pieced center; press seams toward M strips.

Step 5. Join two each H and I squares to make a corner unit as shown in Figure 6; press seams toward H and in one direction. Repeat for four corner units.

Figure 6

Step 6. Sew a corner unit to each end of the N strips referring to the Placement Diagram for positioning; press seams toward N.

Step 7. Sew a strip to the top and bottom of the pieced center to complete the top; press seams toward strips.

Step 8. Complete the quilt referring to Completing Your Quilt on page 175. ★

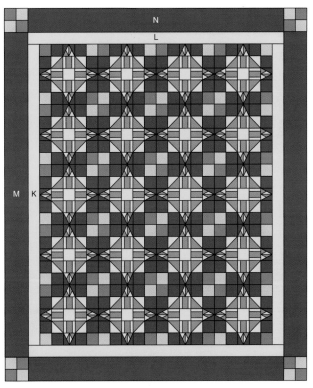

Four-Patch Galaxy
Placement Diagram 78" x 93"

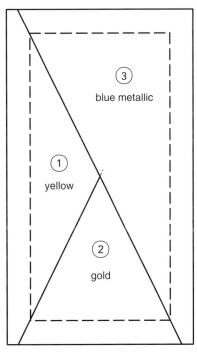

Paper-Piecing Pattern A
Make 80 copies

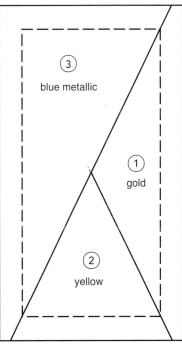

Paper-Piecing Pattern B
Make 80 copies

Zuma Star
9" x 9" Block

DESIGN BY
LINDA MILLER

Zuma Sky

Try this unique method of preparing paper patterns to make this beautiful throw.

Project Specifications
Skill Level: Intermediate
Quilt Size: 54" x 63"
Block Size: 9" x 9"
Number of Blocks: 20

Fabric & Batting
- ½ yard purple mottled batik
- ½ yard magenta mottled batik
- 1¼ yards purple dot batik
- 1⅞ yards blue mottled batik
- 1⅞ yards green dot batik
- 2 yards blue/green print batik
- Backing 60" x 69"
- Batting 60" x 69"

Supplies & Tools
- All-purpose thread to match fabrics
- Quilting thread
- Tissue paper
- Basic sewing tools and supplies

Cutting
Step 1. Cut (16) 4" by fabric width strips each blue mottled (A) and green dot (B); subcut strips into (160) 4" A and B squares.
Step 2. Cut eight 5" by fabric width strips purple dot; subcut strips into (80) 4" C rectangles.
Step 3. Prepare a template for D using pattern given; cut as directed on the piece.
Step 4. Cut six 2½" by fabric width strips purple mottled. Join strips on short ends to make one long strip; press seams open. Subcut strips into two 53" E strips and two 44" F strips.
Step 5. Cut two 7½" x 67" G strips and two 7½" x 58" H strips along the length of the blue/green print.
Step 6. Cut four 2¼"-wide strips along the length of the blue/green print for binding.

Completing the Blocks
Step 1. Make paper copies of Foundation 1 and 2 units as directed with patterns; stitch units using traditional paper-piecing methods referring to the General Instructions or refer to sidebar Precision

With Tissue Paper for designer's special paper-piecing technique (pages 150 and 151).

Step 2. Sew D to Foundation 1 along the short top edge as shown in Figure 1, stopping stitching at the end of the seam allowance as marked on foundation paper, again referring to Figure 1; press seam toward D.

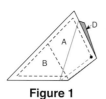

Figure 1

Step 3. Stitch the D-Foundation 1 unit to Foundation 2 along the edge of pieces A and C, pivoting D as necessary at angled edge as shown in Figure 2 to complete a block quarter as shown in Figure 3; press seams toward D. Repeat for four block quarters.

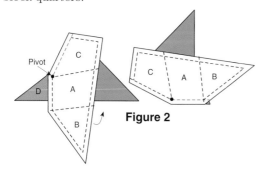

Figure 2

Step 4. Join two block quarters to complete half the block as shown in Figure 4; repeat for two halves.

Press seams in one direction. Join the halves to complete one block, again referring to Figure 4; press seams in one direction. Repeat for 20 blocks. Do not remove paper.

Figure 3

Figure 4

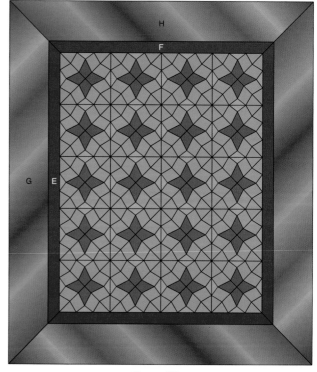

Zuma Sky
Placement Diagram
54" x 63"

Completing the Top

Step 1. Join four blocks to make a row; press seams in one direction. Repeat for five rows.

Step 2. Join the rows to complete the pieced center; press seams in one direction.

Step 3. Center and sew an E strip to opposite long sides and an F strip to the top and bottom of the pieced center, mitering corners. Trim excess fabric at mitered corners to ¼"; press seams open.

Step 4. Center and sew a G strip to opposite long sides and an H strip to the top and bottom of the pieced center, mitering corners. Trim excess fabric at mitered corners to ¼"; press seams open to complete the quilt top.

Step 5. Remove all paper foundations.

Step 6. Complete the quilt referring to Completing Your Quilt on page 175. ★

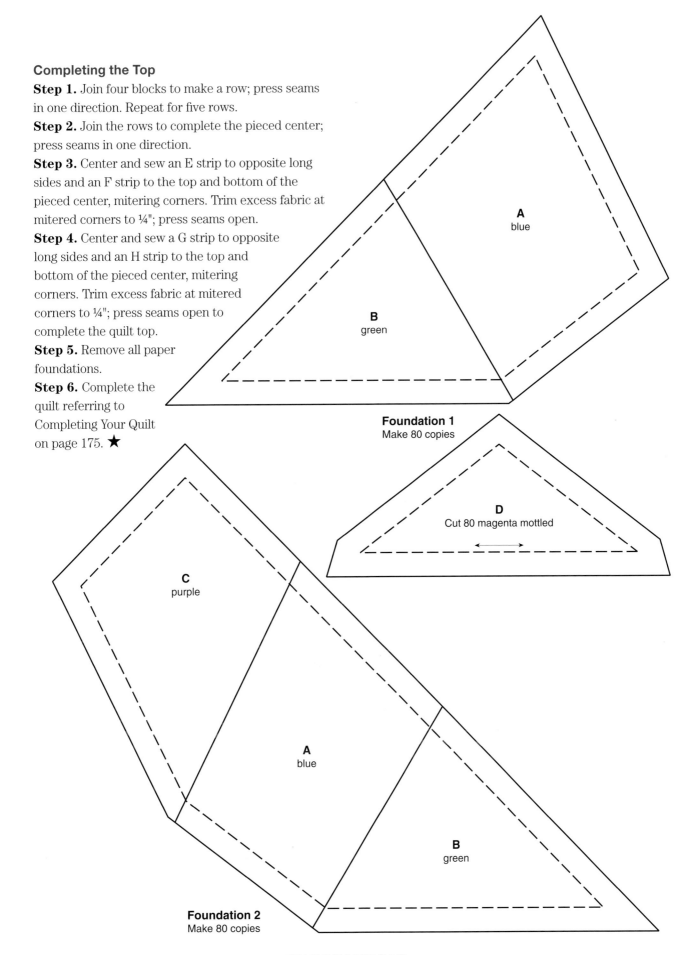

A
blue

B
green

Foundation 1
Make 80 copies

D
Cut 80 magenta mottled

C
purple

A
blue

B
green

Foundation 2
Make 80 copies

Precision With Tissue Paper

I decided to perfect my star points by using paper piecing. I always hated this technique, but I hate my pointless stars even more! With a few minor adjustments, paper piecing can really be the answer to perfect seams. I never liked all the paper and how cumbersome it got while trying to sew all the seams together. Instead of easy-tear foundation paper that you buy at a quilt shop, I use regular tissue paper or a very lightweight vellum. Not only can you see through it, but it is really easy to tear (the tissue more so than the vellum). Also, instead of printing out every copy of my pattern, I only print out a few and use them as templates. Here's how it works.

Step 1. Print out or copy a few copies of the paper-piecing patterns.

Step 2. Place a copy of the paper-piecing pattern on top of 20–30 layers of tissue and, without any thread in the machine, stitch the design outline (Photo 1).

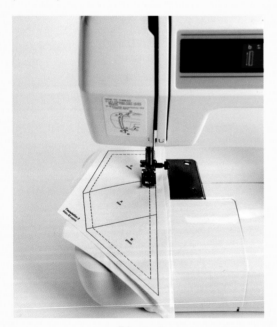

Photo 1

Step 3. Stitch along all other lines on the paper-piecing pattern to make tissue-paper patterns (Photo 2). These perforated lines can be seen from both sides of the paper and eliminate holding up to a light source or guessing where to place the fabric pieces. Continue until you have 80 copies of each foundation pattern.

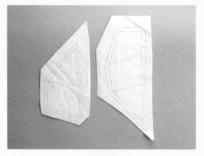

Photo 2

Step 4. Select a Foundation 1 tissue-paper pattern. Place fabric A and B right sides together with fabric A on top. Place the paper pattern on top with the layered squares under section A and one edge of layered squares extending ¼" into section B (Photo 3).

Photo 3

Step 5. Stitch on the line between sections A and B, sewing from edge to edge on the paper pattern (Photo 4). The tissue paper makes it possible to see the seam allowance through the paper without guessing. You may use chain stitching to prepare lots of pieces in an assembly-line fashion. By beginning with the fabric extended ¼" over the seam line, you do not have to trim later. Eliminating the trimming and using assembly-line stitching saves lots of time.

Photo 4

Step 6. Press fabric B over to cover section B to complete the pieced section (Photo 5). Trim excess fabric and paper around outside using outer perforated lines as a guide.

Photo 5

Step 7. Select a Foundation 2 tissue-paper pattern. Begin the same as in Step 4 for Foundation 1 to stitch fabrics A and B. Fold back the tissue on the line between A and C; trim fabric A to extend ¼" beyond this line. Look at the sample for Foundation 2 (Photo 6). Fabric C should be placed with a 5" edge aligned with the A pieces and extending 1" below the long straight edge of the pattern.

Photo 6

Step 8. Test-stitch the A-C section, fold C over and finger-press to be sure the piece covers the entire C section. If the placement is correct, complete the remaining Foundation 2 units.

Step 9. After all units are complete, trim excess around outside using perforated lines as a guide (Photo 7). Pieces are now ready to join to triangle D.

Photo 7

Step 10. Because of its odd shape, D is tricky to fit between Foundations 1 and 2. Begin by joining the proper side of D to Foundation 1, stopping stitching at the A corner seam line (Photo 8). Press seam toward D.

Photo 8

Step 11. With Foundation 2 on top, match the seam lines of A on Foundation 1 and C on Foundation 2, adjusting fabric to keep edges aligned; stitch with Foundation 2 on top, beginning at the seam line at the point of C and stitching to the outside edge of the pattern. Because the paper is on the entire foundation piece, it stabilizes the D triangle and allows the entire unit to keep its shape (Photo 9). Press the unit flat with seams toward D.

Photo 9

Step 12. Join four of these units to complete one block, matching seam lines.

Step 13. Do not remove the paper until the entire quilt top is complete. ★

DESIGN BY
BETH WHEELER

Kaleidoscope Stars

Try this star design that is neither pieced nor appliquéd, but printed on fabric on your ink-jet printer.

Project Specifications
Skill Level: Advanced
Quilt Size: 34" x 50"
Block Size: 14½" x 14½"
Number of Blocks: 6

Fabric & Batting
- ⅝ yard multicolor mottled
- ¾ yard green leaf print
- Backing 40" x 56"
- Batting 40" x 56"

Supplies & Tools
- Neutral color all-purpose thread
- Clear nylon monofilament
- Rayon thread in coordinating and contrasting colors
- 24 (8½" x 11") sheets pretreated ink-jet fabric
- Floral photos or purchased images on CD (Melissa Saylor CD used on sample)
- Computer with photo-editing, painting or drawing software
- Ink-jet printer
- Basic sewing tools and supplies

Project Notes
- Software such as Adobe PhotoShop, PhotoShop Elements, PaintShop Pro, Illustrator, Freehand, Picture This! and others make it possible to manipulate photos or artwork.
- Some programs have a kaleidoscope filter already installed (such as PaintShop Pro) while others (such as PhotoShop) have free plug-ins available to add functionality (such as the kaleidoscope filter). Check the manufacturer's Web site for free plug-ins or links to third-party plug-ins.
- Kaleider is a fun stand-alone kaleidoscope software application that you can try for free before purchasing. This program works with Windows 98, NT and XP (http://www.whizical.com).
- If you are working on a Mac, the tile feature is not supported in OSX. To work around this, use an OS9-native software application to manipulate and print the image.
- Note how one original can create very different looking kaleidoscopic images simply by changing the cropping or orientation of the original artwork as shown in Figures 1–18 on pages 154, 155 and 156.
- A ¼" seam allowance is used throughout, unless otherwise indicated.
- Feel free to make all blocks alike if you wish, or do as we did and make a different kaleidoscope star for each block.

How To Build Your 8-Pointed Star Kaleidoscope Manually
Step 1. Choose a suitable photograph (see Figure 19, page 157); your print should be as vivid as possible.
Step 2. Manipulate the photo with artistic filters, if desired (Figure 20, page 157).
Step 3. Size the photo to 8" x 10".
Step 4. Choose a portion of the image to crop for the star; crop (Figure 21, page 157).

Figure 1
Original artwork used for sample,
Spring Basket, from Melissa
Saylor Crafter's Images™ CD.

Figure 2
Original crop

 =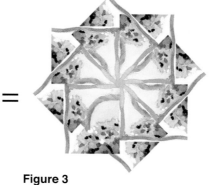

Figure 3
PhotoShop 8-point Kaleidoscope action
applied to the crop to create block motif.

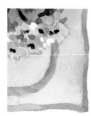

Figure 4
The crop is rotated
180 degrees.

Figure 5
The rotated crop has been
flipped horizontally (also called
mirror image or reflected).

Figure 6
PhotoShop 8-point Kaleidoscope
action has been applied to
rotated-and-flipped crop to
create the block motif.

Figure 7
Original artwork, Delphinium,
from Melissa Saylor Crafter's
Images™ CD.

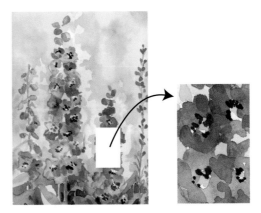

Figure 8
A section of the artwork was cropped.

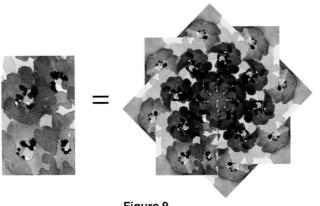

Figure 9
PhotoShop 8-point Kaleidoscope action has
been applied to the crop to create a block.

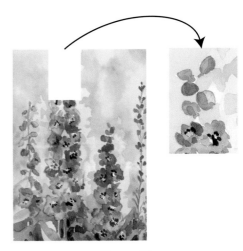

Figure 10
A second crop was taken from the same design.

Figure 11
The crop was rotated 180 degrees and PhotoShop 8-point
Kaleidoscope action was applied to create a block motif.

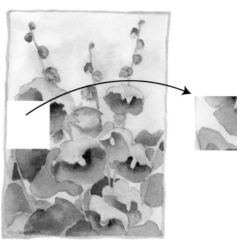

Figure 12
Original artwork, Hollyhocks, from Melissa Saylor Crafter's Images CD.

Figure 13
A section of the artwork was cropped.

Figure 14
PhotoShop 8-point Kaleidoscope action was applied to the crop to create a block motif.

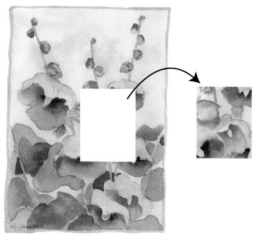

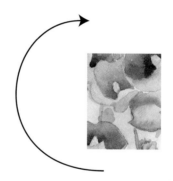

Figure 15
A second image was cropped from the Hollyhock design.

Figure 16
The second crop was rotated 180 degrees.

Figure 17
The block was created using the PhotoShop 8-point Kaleidoscope actions applied.

Figure 18
The same artwork, same crop with PhotoShop 10-point Kaleidoscope actions applied.

Figure 19
Original photo.

Figure 20
Manipulated photo.

Figure 21
Photo with cropped section.

Step 5. Copy the cropped portion and place on a new 8½" x 11" art board (document) as shown in Figure 22.

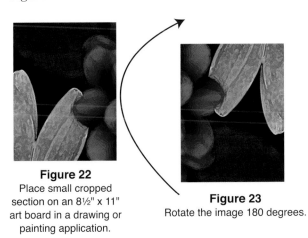

Figure 22
Place small cropped section on an 8½" x 11" art board in a drawing or painting application.

Figure 23
Rotate the image 180 degrees.

Step 6. If desired, rotate the image for maximum impact as the center motif of the star develops (Figure 23); copy.

Step 7. Paste an exact copy of the original cropped portion on the art board beside the original as shown in Figure 24.

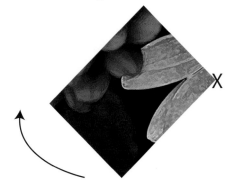

Original   Copy

Figure 24
Make an exact copy.

Step 8. Rotate the lower left corner clockwise 45 degrees as shown in Figure 25.

X

Figure 25
Rotate lower left corner
of the copy 45 degrees.

Step 9. Tuck the rotated copy underneath the original. You'll be working in a circular pattern around a center point, as in Figure 26.

X

Figure 26
Tuck the rotated copy under the original.

Step 10. Make a third copy; rotate the lower left corner clockwise 90 degrees as shown in Figure 27. Tuck the third copy underneath the second (Figure 28).

Figure 27
Make another copy; rotate 90 degrees.

Figure 28
Tuck the rotated copy under the original.

Figure 29
Rotate the fourth copy 135 degrees.

Step 11. Make a fourth copy; rotate 135 degrees clockwise (Figure 29). Tuck underneath the third.
Step 12. The fifth copy is rotated 180 degrees; tuck under the fourth (Figure 30).

Figure 30
Rotate the fifth copy 180 degrees.

Step 13. The sixth copy is rotated 225 degrees; tuck under the fifth (Figure 31).

Figure 31
Rotate the sixth copy 225 degrees.

Step 14. The seventh copy is rotated 270 degrees; tuck under the sixth (Figure 32).

Figure 32
Rotate the seventh copy 270 degrees of 8 in place.
The position for the eighth copy is indicated by
the white rectangle (one corner visible).

Step 15. The last copy is rotated 315 degrees and tucked under the seventh (Figure 33).

Creating Photo Blocks
Step 1. Choose desired artwork from the Melissa Saylor CD, or a favorite floral photo of your own.
Step 2. Follow the instructions with your software application to create the kaleidoscopic image, or refer to How To Build Your 8-Pointed Star Kaleidoscope Manually to create your own.

Figure 33
The manually created 8-point star is complete.

Step 3. Enlarge or reduce the artwork to 8" square on an 8½" x 11" art board (some applications refer to it as "document"). Position in the center of the art board as shown in Figure 34.

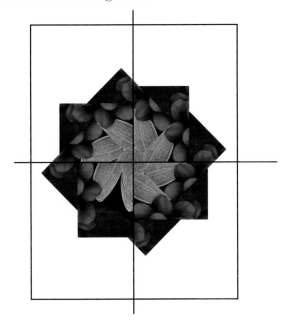

Figure 34
Enlarge or reduce to 8" square. Position in the center of the 8½" x 11" art board.

Step 4. Refer to your printer software (the driver that enables the computer and printer to communicate). There is a feature somewhere (usually in the layout dialog box) that allows the image to be enlarged and automatically divided into segments. Some printer manufacturers call this "tiling" while others call it "postering." Choose the 2 x 2 setting. This will divide the image into four sheets—two sheets across and two down (see Figure 35). Print

the kaleidoscopic star on paper first to ensure desired placement, resolution, contrast and saturation. When you are satisfied with the reproduction, print on fabric (refer to manufacturer's directions for printing tips and directions).

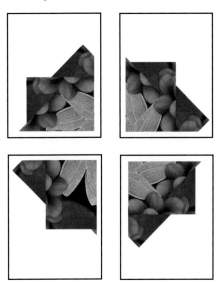

Figure 35
The printer's tiling feature automatically enlarges the image, divides it into 4 pieces, and prints each piece on separate sheets of paper or fabric with an automatic seam allowance.

Step 5. Allow the ink to dry. Separate the fabric from the paper backing.
Step 6. Position the two upper quadrants together, with right sides facing, on a light table or flat window. **Note:** *Light coming through the glass will help you align the pieces.* Stitch together as shown in Figure 36,

Figure 36

with neutral color all-purpose thread in machine top and bobbin. Repeat with two lower quadrants. Press seam allowance open to reduce bulk.

Step 7. Stitch upper and lower halves together (Figure 37); press seam allowance open. Repeat for six blocks.

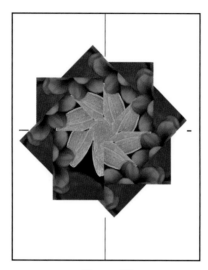

Figure 37

Step 8. Rinse fabric and dry, according to manufacturer's directions.

Step 9. Trim blocks to 15" x 15" as shown in Figure 38.

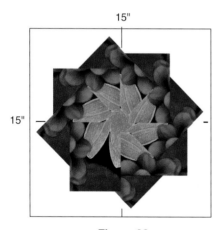

Figure 38

Cutting Instructions for Quilt

Step 1. Cut seven 2" x 15" A strips multicolor mottled.

Step 2. Cut two 2" x 2" B squares green leaf print.

Step 3. Cut three 1¼" by fabric width strips green leaf print. Join strips on short ends to make one long strip; press seams open. Subcut strip into two 47" C strips.

Step 4. Cut two 1¼" x 32½" D strips green leaf print.

Step 5. Cut three 1½" by fabric width strips multicolor mottled. Join strips on short ends to make one long strip; press seams open. Subcut strip into two 48½" E strips.

Step 6. Cut two 1½" x 34½" F strips multicolor mottled.

Step 7. Cut five 2¼" by fabric width strips green leaf print for binding.

Completing the Quilt Top

Step 1. Join two blocks with A to make a block row; press seams toward A. Repeat for three block rows.

Step 2. Join two A strips with B to complete a sashing row; press seams toward A. Repeat for two sashing rows.

Step 3. Join the block rows with the sashing rows to complete the pieced center; press seams toward sashing rows.

Kaleidoscope Stars
Placement Diagram
34" x 50"

Step 4. Sew C to opposite long sides and D to the top and bottom of the pieced center; press seams toward C and D.

Step 5. Sew E to opposite long sides and F to the top and bottom of the pieced center; press seams toward E and F to complete the top.

Completing the Quilt

Step 1. Sandwich batting between the completed top and prepared backing piece; pin or baste layers together to hold flat.

Step 2. Prepare sewing machine with clear nylon monofilament in the upper machine. Fit the machine with a walking foot or quilting foot. Quilt ¼" away from seam allowances along sashing and borders.

Step 3. Replace the clear nylon monofilament with rayon thread in a color to coordinate with the quilt block in the top and rayon thread in a color to coordinate with the backing in the bobbin. Drop the feed dogs and fit the machine with a free-motion or darning foot.

Step 4. Stitch along lines of the star blocks to add color and texture (thread painting).

Step 5. Replace upper thread with clear nylon monofilament thread and work lots of meander quilting in the white background of the blocks.

Step 6. Remove basting; press quilt well with steam iron, using a press cloth to protect the quilt from any residue on the iron's soleplate.

Step 7. When quilting is complete, remove pins or basting; trim batting and backing edges even with quilt top.

Step 8. Join binding strips on short ends to make one long strip; press seams open.

Step 9. Fold binding strip in half with wrong sides together along length; press.

Step 10. Sew binding strip to quilt top with raw edges even, mitering corners and overlapping ends. Turn binding to the back side; hand- or machine-stitch in place to finish. ★

DESIGN BY
CHRIS MALONE

Yo-Yo Star Table Topper

Star shapes are appliquéd to a background made of yo-yos to make an unusual table topper.

Project Specifications

Skill Level: Beginner
Table Topper Size: 20" x 16"

Fabric & Batting

- 1½" x 20" strip neutral-color fabric for hanging sleeve
- Assorted red, green, blue and tan scraps
- ⅜ yard gold mottled
- ¾ yard quilter's fleece

Supplies & Tools

- All-purpose thread to match fabrics
- Quilting thread
- 5 (⅞") shank buttons
- Permanent fabric adhesive
- Basic sewing tools and supplies

Instructions

Step 1. Prepare templates for the circles using patterns given; cut as directed.

Step 2. Cut a 1" x 1" scrap of fabric to match each fabric circle.

Step 3. Center a fleece circle on the wrong side of a fabric circle; secure in place with a dot of permanent fabric adhesive.

Step 4. Center a 1" x 1" scrap square to match the fabric circle on the fleece; secure in place with a dot of permanent fabric adhesive. ***Note:** This scrap covers the quilter's fleece so it does not show in the center of the finished yo-yo.*

Step 5. Thread a needle with a double strand of thread to match the fabric circle. Turn under the edges all around ⅛" and finger-press to hold.

Step 6. Sew a line of gathering stitches around the folded edge as shown in Figure 1; pull up stitches tightly with right side of fabric facing out, pushing the hole to the center, again referring to Figure 1. Run the thread to the back of the yo-yo; knot and clip to complete one yo-yo. Repeat for 80 yo-yos.

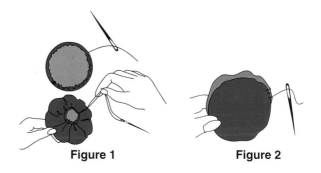

Figure 1   **Figure 2**

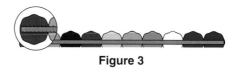

Figure 3

Step 7. Arrange yo-yos in eight rows of 10 yo-yos each.

Step 8. To join, hold two yo-yos together with gathered sides facing; take 3 or 4 small stitches right at the edge of the circle as shown in Figure 2. Unfold the pair and add a third yo-yo in the same manner; repeat with 10 yo-yos to complete a row (Figure 3).

Repeat to make eight rows; join rows in the same manner to complete the yo-yo table topper base.

Step 9. Prepare template for star shapes using patterns given.

Step 10. To make star appliqués, fold the gold mottled fabric in half with right sides together; trace three large and two small stars on one side.

Step 11. Layer the traced fabric with the quilter's fleece; pin. Sew all around on traced lines through all layers; cut out ⅛" from stitched seams. Clip into corners and trim points; trim fleece very close to stitching.

Step 12. Cut a slash through the top layer of fabric only; turn star shapes right side out through opening. Press. Slipstitch the opening closed. Topstitch ¼" from outer edge of star all around with matching thread.

Step 13. To cover each button, fold edge of button circle and hand-sew as for yo-yo. Place a shank button in the center of the fabric and pull stitches tightly around the shank. Knot thread; sew button to the center of a star.

Step 14. Referring to the Placement Diagram and photo of the topper, arrange the stars on the yo-yo base; apply dots of permanent fabric adhesive to the back of the star shapes where they touch a yo-yo to complete the table topper. ★

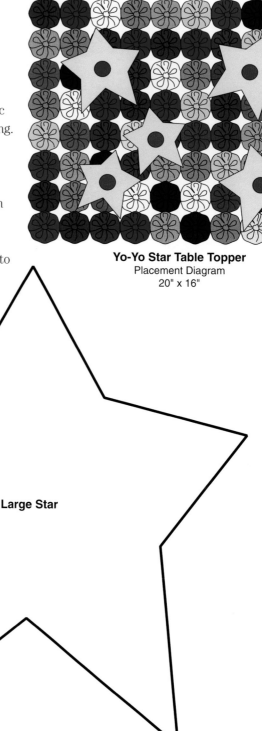

Yo-Yo Star Table Topper
Placement Diagram
20" x 16"

Large Star

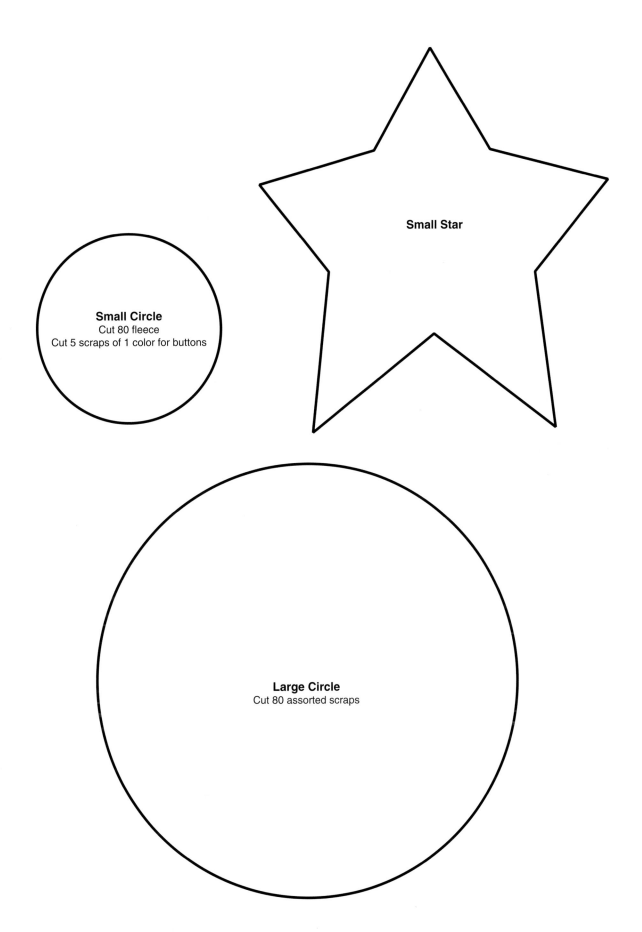

Small Star

Small Circle
Cut 80 fleece
Cut 5 scraps of 1 color for buttons

Large Circle
Cut 80 assorted scraps

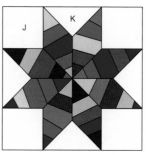

Morning Star
12" x 12" Block
Make 20

Appliqué Flower
17" x 17" Block
Make 4

DESIGN BY
CHRISTINE SCHULTZ

Morning Star

Use lots of scraps to create the star points of the outer blocks in this stunning appliquéd-and-pieced star-design quilt.

Project Specifications
Skill Level: Intermediate
Quilt Size: 102" x 102"
Block Size: 12" x 12" and 17" x 17"
Number of Blocks: 20 and 4

Fabric & Batting
- Assorted print scraps
- 1 fat quarter each lavender mottled and tan, brick red, turquoise and green prints
- ⅓ yard black solid
- ⅓ yard brown print
- ½ yard purple print
- ½ yard teal print
- ⅝ yard black print
- ⅝ yard gold mottled
- 1½ yards total assorted white-with-black prints
- 1¾ yards white print
- 5¾ yards rust print

- Backing 108" x 108"
- Batting 108" x 108"

Supplies & Tools
- All-purpose thread to match fabrics
- Quilting thread
- Green 6-strand embroidery floss
- Freezer paper
- Basic sewing tools and supplies

Cutting
Step 1. Refer to Completing the Appliqué Flower Blocks for appliqué cutting instructions.
Step 2. Refer to Completing the Morning Star Blocks to create strip-pieced J diamonds.
Step 3. Cut a 146" length rust print; cut two 5½"-wide strips along length. Cut strips into four 5½" x 72" I strips.
Step 4. Cut the remainder of rust print length into

three 9⅛" x 146" strips; subcut strips into 36 N triangles as shown in Figure 1.

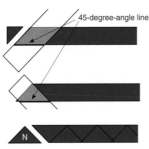

Figure 1

Step 5. Cut four brown print, five purple print, six each gold mottled and teal print, seven black print and eight rust print 2½" by fabric width strips for star-point pieces.

Step 6. Cut four 17½" x 17½" G squares white print; fold and crease to mark the diagonal centers.

Step 7. Cut one 25¼" x 25¼" square white print; cut the square in half on both diagonals to make four H triangles as shown in Figure 2.

Figure 2

Step 8. For each Morning Star block, choose a white-with-black print and cut four 4" x 4" J squares and one 6¼" x 6¼" K square. Cut the K square on both diagonals to make four K triangles. Repeat for 20 blocks. *Note: The sample uses a different white-with-black print fabric in each block.*

Step 9. Cut four 9⅜" x 9⅜" squares rust print; cut each square on one diagonal to make a total of eight M triangles.

Step 10. Cut ten 2¼" by fabric width strips rust print for binding.

Completing the Appliqué Flower Blocks

Step 1. Transfer complete appliqué shape to the G squares referring to the block drawing for positioning and using creased lines as guides for centering design.

Step 2. Cut a freezer-paper piece for each appliqué shape as directed on patterns for number to cut. *Note: You will need a total of 20 small leaf shapes, four plus eight plus eight.* Use the inner solid line to cut the freezer-paper shapes for the large leaf, bud,

bud center, flower and flower center shapes.

Step 3. Iron the freezer-paper shapes onto the wrong side of the fabrics as directed on patterns for color. Cut out shapes ³⁄₁₆" beyond the edge of the paper piece.

Step 4. Turn under edges of shapes over the freezer-paper shapes; hand-stitch shapes, except small leaves and berries, to the right side of the black solid as shown in Figure 3. *Note: Leave edges unstitched where one piece overlaps another, again referring to Figure 3.*

Figure 3   **Figure 4**

Step 5. Trim away the black solid from beneath the appliquéd shapes, leaving a ³⁄₁₆" seam allowance; remove freezer paper.

Step 6. Cut larger freezer-paper shapes for the large leaf, bud, bud center, flower and flower center using the outer solid lines on the pattern and referring to the pattern for number to cut of each.

Step 7. Position the larger freezer-paper shapes under the matching appliquéd piece on the wrong side of the black solid as shown in Figure 4. *Note: A light source helps position the freezer paper to leave an even amount of black around the appliquéd shape when complete.*

Step 8. Cut out fabric pieces around freezer-paper shapes leaving a ³⁄₁₆" black solid edge all around; turn edge over freezer paper and press. Remove freezer paper.

Step 9. Appliqué all shapes to the G squares in numerical order referring to the pattern for order numbers and Figure 5 for positioning.

Figure 5

Step 10. Using 3 strands green embroidery floss, stem-stitch berry stems to complete the blocks.

Completing the Star Center

Step 1. Arrange the 2½"-wide fabric strips together in sets in the following combinations and order: Set A—gold, brown, teal, rust, yellow and black; Set B—brown, teal, rust, gold, black and purple; Set C—teal, rust, gold, black, purple and rust; Set D—rust, gold, black, purple, rust and teal; Set E—gold, black, purple, rust, teal and brown; Set F: black, purple,

rust, teal, brown and black.

Step 2. Sew strips with right sides together along length in pairs, off-setting strips 2" as shown in Figure 6; press seams open, being careful not to distort the strip set. Sew strip pairs together into full strip sets, offsetting pairs 2".

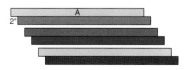

Figure 6

Step 3. Lay the A strip set flat on a cutting mat with first color listed at the bottom. Position a rotary ruler so the 45-degree-angle line is aligned with the bottom edge of the strip set as shown in Figure 7.

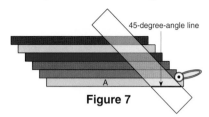

Figure 7

Step 4. Trim the right end of the strip set at a 45-degree angle; turn the cutting mat around 180 degrees so that the first strip in the set is at the top and the trimmed end is to the left as shown in Figure 8.

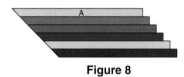

Figure 8

Step 5. Align the 45-degree-angle line on the ruler with the bottom edge of the strip set; measure and then cut 2½" from the left edge as shown in Figure 9. Continue cutting in this way until you have cut eight pieced strips. Repeat with each strip set; label strips from each strip set with the letter of the strip set to avoid confusion.

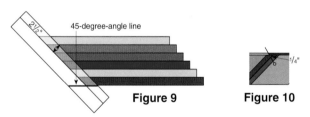

Figure 9   **Figure 10**

Step 6. Sew an A strip to a B strip, pinning at seams as shown in Figure 10; press seam open. Repeat for strips C and D and E and F. Join the pairs in alphabetical order to create one star point as shown in Figure 11; press seams open. Repeat for eight star points.

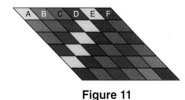

Figure 11

Step 7. To complete the center, join the star points in pairs, pinning at seam intersections as shown in Figure 12, starting and stopping stitching at the ends of the seam, not at the end of the pieces, as shown in Figure 13; press seams open. Join the pairs to make halves; join halves to complete the star design. Press seams open.

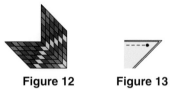

Figure 12   **Figure 13**

Step 8. Set in H triangles between alternating star points, starting stitching at the outside edge and stitching to the center, stopping stitching at the end of the seam, not the end of the fabric, as in Figure 13 in Step 7; press seams toward H. Repeat with Appliqué Flower blocks in each corner to complete the quilt center; press seams toward Appliqué Flower blocks.

Completing the Morning Star Blocks

Step 1. Cut assorted print scraps into random-width strips no narrower than 1". ***Note:*** *Strips may be straight or angled along length.*

Step 2. Join strips in random order and press to make pieced yardage of about 18" x 22".

Step 3. Prepare a template for L. Place the template on the pieced yardage as shown in Figure 14. Place a ruler with one edge aligned on the edge of L and trim along the ruler edge, again referring to Figure 14.

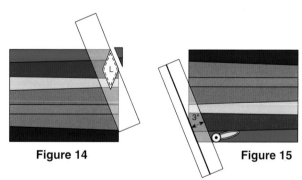

Figure 14   **Figure 15**

Step 4. Place the 3" line on the ruler on the trimmed edge of the pieced yardage as shown in Figure 15; trim along edge of ruler to cut a 3" strip. Repeat to cut strips across the pieced yardage.

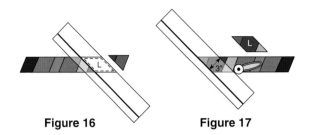

Figure 16　　　　**Figure 17**

Step 5. Place the L template on one strip as shown in Figure 16; trim off end along edge of template, again referring to Figure 16.

Step 6. Cut 3" segments along length of strip to make L pieces as shown in Figure 17; repeat with all strips.

Step 7. Continue to piece yardage to cut a total of 160 L pieces. ***Note:*** *You will need to piece at least eight 18" x 22" sections.*

Step 8. Join L in pairs, then halves and then full stars and press as in Step 7 in Completing the Star Center.

Step 9. Set in J and K pieces and press as for H triangles and Appliqué Flower blocks in Step 8 in Completing the Star Center.

Completing the Quilt Top

Step 1. Center and sew an I strip to each side of the pieced center, mitering corners; trim corner seam to ¼" and press mitered seam open as shown in Figure 18.

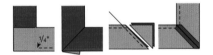

Figure 18

Step 2. Join four Morning Star blocks with eight N triangles and two M triangles to make a side border strip as shown in Figure 19; press seams away from blocks. Repeat for two strips.

Figure 19

Step 3. Sew a side border strip to opposite sides of the pieced center; press seams toward M.

Step 4. Join six Morning Star blocks with 10 N triangles and two M triangles to make a top border strip as shown in Figure 20; repeat for a bottom border strip. Press seams away from blocks.

Figure 20

Step 5. Sew the top and bottom rows to the pieced center; join side and top and bottom border strips at corners as shown in Figure 21; press seams toward O.

Step 6. Complete the quilt referring to Completing Your Quilt on page 175. ★

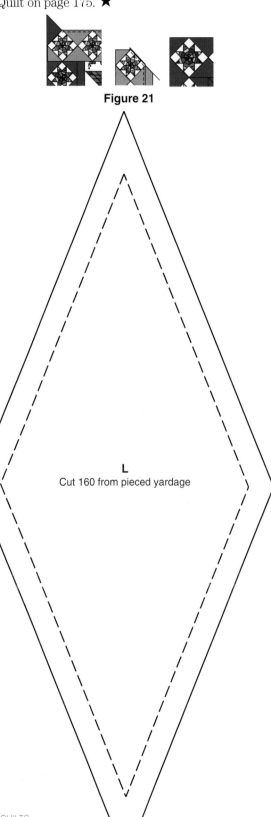

Figure 21

L
Cut 160 from pieced yardage

Berry
Cut 40
lavender
mottled

Bud Center
Cut 4
gold
mottled

①

Bud
Cut 4 brick red print

②

Place line on fold

③

Large Leaf
Cut 8 teal print
(reverse 4)

Match to berry stem here

Flower
Cut 4
turquoise print

④

⑤

Flower Center
Cut 4 tan print

⑥

Small Leaf
Cut 4 teal tonal & 8
each teal & green prints

Flower Motif

⑦

⑧

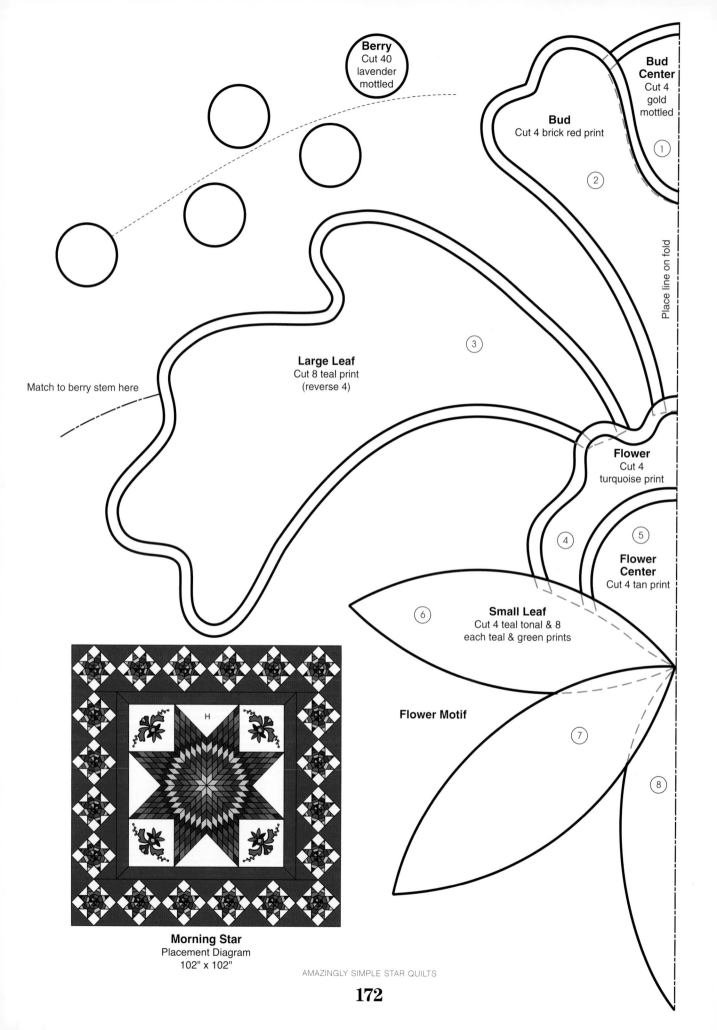

Morning Star
Placement Diagram
102" x 102"

General Instructions

There are many wonderful books on the market that include very specific instructions for all facets of quiltmaking. This book is intended to be a pattern book, not a how-to book for quilters.

There are a few bits of basic information you should be aware of. Use a ¼" seam allowance for all piecing unless otherwise specified. Most patterns include rotary-cutting instructions wherever possible. Templates are given where the use of quick-cutting instructions is not feasible.

Quick-piecing methods are recommended to make best use of time and resources.

Specific instructions follow for paper piecing because many patterns in this book use this method. General instructions are also given for completing your quilt.

Basic Paper Piecing

Blocks with many different shapes joined with straight seams are good candidates for paper piecing. Rather than make lots of templates that are used only once, the fabric is stitched onto a paper foundation for the block or block section. Full-size patterns for each section are included for paper-pieced blocks. Basic information and hints for paper piecing are given here.

Choosing Foundation Paper

• Always remember that your stitched piece will be the reverse image of the printed pattern. You will place the fabric on the back, unprinted side of the paper pattern. Often patterns must be traced or made in reverse to be used as paper-piecing patterns. The patterns given here have already been reversed to allow easy photocopying or tracing.

• Choose paper for the patterns that will not tear as you stitch, but that will tear away easily when all stitching is complete. Choose paper that will allow you to see through from the back to the printed side with only the light from your sewing machine to assist you. It does not have to be transparent.

You may purchase paper specially designed for paper piecing. Most can be used in a photocopier or computer printer. It is usually translucent enough to allow you to see the stitching lines from the back side, and it can be removed when your block is complete without damaging the stitches.

Of course, you may use other paper that you have on hand or that is readily available. Tracing paper, multi-use paper and photocopier paper are possible choices. The large sheets of lightweight buff-colored paper used for packing work well and help with recycling. Its porous quality allows the pattern lines to bleed through to the fabric side, making placement easier. It tears away easily without pulling the stitches. The large size accommodates 12" or larger blocks without combining sheets.

Test paper for stitching stability by sewing a line with your machine set at 18–20 stitches per inch. The stitches should perforate the paper without creating a cut along the stitching line. Now, try to tear the paper away from the line of stitches. It should come away easily without stretching or distorting the stitches and without leaving shreds of paper behind.

Preparing Patterns

• Paper-piecing patterns may be photocopied for stitching. Check that the photocopied image is the same size as the original. Many photocopiers distort the image. A change in size, however slight, may make a difference in the overall piecing of your block. Also, check the photocopied pattern to be sure the ink will not come off on your iron when pressing pieces while sewing.

• To make the patterns by hand, use a permanent pen or pencil to trace the patterns exactly. Beware of any ink that may run. In heavily stitched areas, the paper foundation may not be entirely removed. Future washing may cause any ink left within the stitching to run.

• Cut out each section, leaving a margin beyond the heavy outer line as shown in Figure 1.

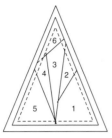

Figure 1

Stitching Patterns

• Begin with a sharp needle in your sewing machine. Shorten your stitch length to 18–20 stitches per inch. This shorter stitch length allows for easy removal of the paper without stretching the stitches.

• Use thread to match fabrics or a neutral color that will blend with all the fabrics.

• Cut a piece of fabric for area 1. The piece should be larger than the area to allow for seam allowance all around the area. If the pattern has unusual-angled shapes or shapes with very long points, it is easier to precut the pieces using a pattern. Make an extra copy of the section pattern and cut it apart on the solid lines as shown in Figure 2. Use each piece to rough-cut a fabric piece as shown in Figure 3. Cut the pieces larger all around than the paper piece to allow for seam allowance and to allow a bit of leeway in arranging the pieces before stitching.

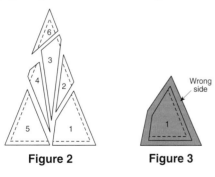

Figure 2   **Figure 3**

• Place fabric to cover area 1 on the paper pattern with wrong side of fabric against the unmarked side of the paper, allowing fabric to extend at least ¼" into adjacent areas as shown in Figure 4.

• Place fabric for area 2 right sides together with fabric 1 on the 1-2 edge as shown in Figure 5; pin along the 1-2 line. Fold fabric 2 over to cover area 2, allowing fabric to extend at least ¼" into adjacent

areas as shown in Figure 6. Adjust fabric if necessary. Unfold fabric 2 to lie flat on fabric 1.

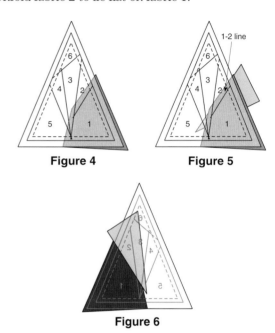

Figure 4   **Figure 5**

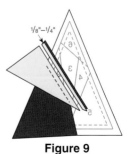

Figure 6

• Flip paper pattern; stitch on the 1-2 line, beginning and ending 2 or 3 stitches into adjacent areas as shown in Figure 7. Stitch to (or beyond) the outside heavy solid line on outer areas as shown in Figure 8.

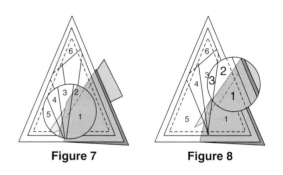

Figure 7   **Figure 8**

• Trim the 1-2 seam allowance to ⅛"–¼" as shown in Figure 9. Fold fabric 2 to cover area 2; lightly press with a warm dry iron.

Figure 9

• Continue to add fabrics in numerical order to cover the paper pattern as shown in Figure 10. Check that each piece will cover its area before stitching. The very short stitches are hard to remove and often cause a tear in the paper pattern. Should this happen, place a small piece of transparent tape over the tear to continue to use the pattern. Do not use this quick fix frequently, as it makes removal of the paper difficult.

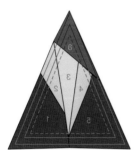

Figure 10

• Pin outside fabric edges to paper pattern. Trim paper and fabric edges even on the outside heavy solid line as shown in Figure 11.

Figure 11

• Place block sections with fabric sides together. Stick a pin through both sections at each end of the dashed seam line to be sure the lines on both sections match as shown in Figure 12. Stitch along the dashed seam lines to join the sections as shown in Figure 13. Remove paper from seam allowance area only. Press seam to one side.

Figure 12   **Figure 13**

• Join all block sections to complete the block.
• Leave paper pattern intact until the block is joined with other quilt pieces.

Completing Your Quilt

Step 1. Sandwich the batting between the completed top and prepared backing; pin or baste layers together to hold. **_Note:_** _If using basting spray to hold layers together, refer to instructions on the product container for use._

Step 2. Quilt as desired by hand or machine; remove pins or basting. Trim excess backing and batting even with quilt top.

Step 3. Join binding strips on short ends to make one long strip. Fold the strip in half along length with wrong sides together; press.

Step 4. Sew binding to quilt edges, mitering corners and overlapping ends. Fold binding to the back side and stitch in place to finish. ★

Special Thanks

We would like to thank the talented quilt designers whose
work is featured in this collection.

Julia Dunn
Twinkling Gold, 30

Sue Harvey
Jewel of the Night, 96
Stars of the Forest, 14
Star Rockets in Flight, 129
The Stars Inside, 124

Sandra Hatch
Circling Stars of the Orient, 103
Spinning Stars, 87
Stars in the Crossroads, 80

Connie Kauffman
Garden Stars, 6
Ocean Stars, 38

Shimmering Stars, 42
Starburst, 19

Dolores Keaton
Ahoya Flowers, 54

Kate Laucomer
Homespun Stars, 138

Chris Malone
Prairie Points Throw, 77
Yo-Yo Star Table Topper, 162

Linda Miller
Fireworks Fancy, 66
Island Sunrise, 45
Zuma Sky, 146

Connie Rand
Four-Patch Galaxy, 142
Plenty of Stars, 10
Shining Stars, 63

Jill Reber
Double Star Baby Quilt, 84
Stars in Flight, 121
Welcome Home, 50

Sue Reeves
Shooting Star, 22

Judith Sandstrom
Filtered Sunlight, 27
Heavenly Stars, 70
Starry Night, 92

Christine Schultz
Back to the Fifties, 116
Morning Star, 166

Julie Weaver
Framed Stars, 112
Grandmother's Stars, 34
Starflowers Quilt, 134
True Colors, 74
Woven Stars, 108

Beth Wheeler
Kaleidoscope Stars, 152

Fabrics & Supplies

Page 6: Garden Stars—Hobbs Heirloom fusible batting. Sulky threads and Triangulations 2.0 Half Square and Quarter Square CD ROM.

Page 10: Plenty of Stars—Forest Fantasy fabric collection from Timeless Treasures, Fairfield Soft Touch cotton batting and Star Machine Quilting Thread from Coats.

Page 14: Stars of the Forest—Bentley's Fat Cat Quarters, Star Machine Quilting Thread from Coats, Fairfield Natural cotton batting and 505 Spray and Fix basting spray.

Page 19: Starburst—Hobbs Heirloom fusible batting.

Page 22: Shooting Star—Pellon Quilter's Grid 1"-grid fusible interfacing.

Page 27: Filtered Sunlight—Fiskars rotary-cutting tools and DMC quilting thread and needles.

Page 34: Grandmother's Stars—Hobbs Thermore batting. Machine-quilted by Michelle Smith.

Page 38: Ocean Stars—Sulky threads, Hobbs Heirloom batting and Triangles on a Roll.

Page 42: Shimmering Stars—Hobbs Heirloom fusible cotton batting and Sulky Blendable thread.

Page 50: Welcome Home—Master Piece 45 Ruler and Static Stickers from Master Piece Products. Sewing machine provided by Pfaff.

Page 63: Shining Stars—Marble Mania, Christmas and Glimmer fabric collection from Timeless Treasures, poly-fil Natural Cotton batting from Fairfield Processing and Star Machine Quilting Thread from Coats.

Page 70: Heavenly Stars—DMC quilting thread and needles and Fiskars rotary-cutting tools.

Page 74: True Colors—Hobbs Thermore batting. Machine-quilted by Michelle Smith.

Page 80: Stars in the Crossroads—Watercolor Meadows fabric collection from Robert Kaufman, Star Machine Quilting Thread from Coats and Fairfield Processing Machine 60/40 Blend batting. Machine-stitched on a BabyLock ellagéo. Machine-quilted by Dianne Hodgkins.

Page 84: Double Star Baby Quilt—Master Piece 45 Ruler and Static Stickers from Master Piece Products and Pfaff sewing machine.

Page 87: Spinning Stars—Wild Iris fabric collection from Northcott, Fairfield Processing Machine 60/40 Blend batting, Star Machine Quilting Thread from Coats and Tri-Rec Tools acrylic templates. Machine-stitched on a BabyLock ellagéo. Machine-quilted by Dianne Hodgkins.

Page 92: Starry Night—DMC quilting thread and needles and Fiskars rotary-cutting tools.

Page 96: Jewel of the Night—Tonga Batiks from Timeless Treasures, Star Machine Quilting Thread from Coats, Fairfield Machine 60/40 Batting and 505 Spray and Fix.

Page 103: Circling Stars of the Orient—Oriental Traditions fabric collection from Robert Kaufman, Star Machine Quilting Thread rom Coats, Tri-Rec Tools acrylic templates and Fairfield Processing Machine 60/40 Blend batting. Machine-stitched on a BabyLock ellagéo. Machine-quilted by Dianne Hodgkins.

Page 108: Woven Stars—Hobbs Thermore batting. Professionally machine-quilted by Michelle Smith.

Page 112: Framed Stars—Coventry Garden fabric collection from P&B Textiles and Thermore batting from Hobbs. Machine-quilted by Michelle Smith.

Page 121: Stars in Flight—Pfaff sewing machine and Master Piece 45 Ruler and Static Stickers from Master Piece Products. Sewing machine provided by Pfaff.

Page 124: The Stars Inside—Tri-Rec Tools acrylic templates, Star Machine Quilting Thread from Coats and Fairfield Processing Machine 60/40 Blend batting. Machine-quilted by Sandy Boobar.

Page 129: Star Rockets in Flight—Heavy Metals and Artisan's Palette fabrics from Northcott, Star Machine Quilting Thread from Coats and Fairfield Processing Machine 60/40 Blend batting. Machine-quilted by Sandy Boobar.

Page 134: Starflowers Quilt—Lite Steam-A-Seam 2 from The Warm Co. and Thermore batting from Hobbs. Machine-quilted by Michelle Smith.

Page 142: Four-Patch Galaxy—Not So Solid, Marble Mania, Imagine and Timeless Christmas Blenders fabric collections from Timeless Treasures, Fairfield Processing Natural Cotton batting, and Star Machine Quilting Thread from Coats. Machine-quilted by Lorraine Sweet.

Page 146: Zuma Sky—Bali Batiks from Hoffman. Machine-quilted by Lillian Lee.

Page 152: Kaleidoscope Stars—Crafter's Images Melissa Saylor artwork CDs and PhotoFabric from Blumenthal Craft.

Page 162: Yo-Yo Star Table Topper—Beacon Fabri-Tac fabric adhesive.